Linda,
You're God's
thing!
Lovin' Jesus
Linda Newton

I Want Something…
Better Than
JEWELS

Books by Linda Newton
Available from Warner Press

12 Ways to Turn Your Pain into Praise

Better Than Jewels

I Want Something...
Better Than
JEWELS

31 Days of Biblical Insight
for a Woman Seeking God

....

Linda Newton

Warner Press

Anderson, Indiana

Coordinator of Publishing & Creative Services
Church of God Ministries, Inc.
PO Box 2420, Anderson, IN 46018-2420
800-848-2464 • www.chog.org

To purchase additional copies of this book, to inquire about distribution, and for all other sales-related matters, please contact:

Warner Press, Inc.
PO Box 2499, Anderson, IN 46018-2499
800-741-7721 • www.warnerpress.org

All Scripture quotations, unless otherwise indicated, are taken from the Holy Bible, New International Version®. NIV®. Copyright © 1973, 1978, 1984 by International Bible Society. Used by permission of Zondervan. All rights reserved.

Scripture quotations marked MSG are taken from *The Message* by Eugene H. Peterson, copyright © 1993, 1994, 1995, 1996, 2000, 2001, 2002. Used by permission of NavPress Publishing Group. All rights reserved.

Scripture quotations marked NLT are taken from the Holy Bible, New Living Translation, copyright © 1996. Used by permission of Tyndale House Publishers, Inc., Wheaton, Illinois 60189. All rights reserved.

Scripture quotations marked NRSV are taken from the New Revised Standard Version Bible, copyright 1989, Division of Christian Education of the National Council of the Churches of Christ in the United States of America. Used by permission. All rights reserved.

Cover and text design by Carolyn Frost.
Edited by Joseph D. Allison and Stephen R. Lewis.

ISBN-13:978-1-59317-369-2

Library of Congress Cataloging-in-Publication Data
Newton, Linda, 1954-
    Better than jewels : 31 days of biblical insight for a woman seeking God / Linda Newton.
        p.   cm.
    ISBN 978-1-59317-369-2 (harcover)
    1. Christian women--Prayers and devotions. 2. Bible. O.T. Proverbs--Meditations.
        I. Title.
    BV4844.N48 2009
    242'.643--dc22   2009001778

Printed in the United States of America.
09 10 11 12 13 14 15 / VP / 10 9 8 7 6 5 4 3 2 1

"For wisdom is better than jewels; and all that you may desire cannot compare with her."

—Proverbs 8:11 NRSV

Day 1: Help

"Let love and faithfulness never leave you; bind them around your neck, write them on the tablet of your heart." (Prov 3:3)

....

Scripture Insight: Have you noticed how fashionable crosses are these days? Especially crosses dangling in the center of big, brightly colored beads? I love bling, so I have several colors and patterns of crosses, each matching different outfits.

Many of us wear crosses as more than just fashion accessories; we wear them as symbols of our faith in Jesus Christ. As the writer of Proverbs notes, we can do even better than this: We can wear divine love like a necklace and demonstrate it to others every chance we get. We can make God look good!

Angel in the Checkout Line

It was one of those days I wished so badly was over, but the end was nowhere in sight. We had just moved into a new house and my to-do list was incredible. With a precocious two-year-old in tow, my day of errands seemed ever longer. Picking out new phones had no interest for my active daughter. Neither did the lengthy debate with folks at the gas company, trying to convince them that the previous owners were terminating their service today and the account needed to be changed to our name now, not next week.

With each stop, Sarah became even more irritable in her boredom. After picking up a prescription for my husband and stopping at the hardware store for picture-hanging gear, we were nearing dinnertime. Both of us were cranky, hot, and tired. My precious blue-eyed bundle seemed inconsolable as I wrestled her into her car seat. I had run out of toys from her diaper bag to entertain her, so now I was fishing in my purse and lobbing anything that might quiet her over the car seat. Over went my checkbook, a handkerchief, even my house keys. "Here, Sweetie. Look what Mommy has. See shiny keys. Sarah loves shiny keys." But nothing calmed her down.

If we had anything at all to eat in our new house, I would have given up on the supermarket altogether. But alas, we didn't—so I managed to maneuver a very unhappy little girl out of her car seat and into the store. By now what little patience Sarah possessed was long gone. She had one nerve left and I was on it. Nothing I did could pacify her.

I entered the grocery store like I was marching into battle. Armed with my list in one hand, pushing a cart with the other, I determined this would be the fastest shopping trip on record. But Sarah's sniveling turned into shrieks. I spotted Scooby Doo on the front of a box of fruit rollups. I rationalized that the snack was fruit and therefore wouldn't be too unhealthy. (Of course, that wasn't true. If I had landed in an aisle next to foot-long Ghirardelli chocolate bars, I probably would have yanked one off the shelf, torn open the wrapper, and handed it to her, just to hush her up.) "Here, Baby. Scooby Doo," I placated.

"Rooby Roo!" she said, imitating her favorite cartoon character as her sobs subsided. It was working. I quickly unwrapped the red-and-green sticky treat and presented it to her. "Eat this, Honey. Mmm, good." Kicking her feet against the cart with delight, she grabbed it from me. I almost responded with, "Say thank you!" but decided I'd save the lesson on manners for another day.

With the determination of a commandant, I powered my cart through the store, tossing in items at record speed. I congratulated myself as I pushed the cart to the next available checker. But I had triumphed too soon. Just then, Sarah came to the end of her fruit roll-up and wanted another one. She wasn't in any mood to bargain. I knew that if I gave her more sugar, we would have to peel her off of the ceiling when we got home. Still, I was considering it.

A kind-faced lady in front of me turned and asked, "Would she let me take her?" Her husband was paying for their groceries, and she seemed to have the time and interest to help.

Caught off guard, I mumbled, "I don't know. Are you sure? She's a sticky mess."

"I'm a seasoned grandma," she beamed, turning to show off her T-shirt covered in children's acrylic handprints, all with names printed next to them. "I have five kids and thirteen grandkids. I can handle one fussy little girl. A crying kid is child's play—no pun intended." We laughed as I pried a sobbing Sarah, whose hair was now festooned with fruit roll-up, from the shopping cart.

"Come and see me," the woman said with a smile as she reached out to my sticky, screaming child.

To my surprise, Sarah reached back. The comforting grandma soothed Sarah as they swayed back and forth in the check-out line while I unloaded my grocery cart onto the counter. "I'm Grandma Ethel," the woman stated.

"That's Sarah and I'm Linda," I replied. By now, Sarah was quiet as a kitten, swaying in Grandma Ethel's arms while I finished paying for my groceries. "I can't tell you how much I appreciate this."

"The pleasure is all mine," Ethel said, squeezing Sarah's face next to hers. As she pulled away, I noticed large dollops of red-and-green fruit roll-up on the dear lady's cheek, neck, and even her hair.

"Sarah got you all sticky," I said apologetically.

"Don't give it a second thought. Isn't being sticky a badge of motherhood? You got to finish your shopping while Sarah and I had a lovely visit."

After saying good-bye, Sarah and I headed for the car. I found myself thanking God for Grandma Ethel, who was willing to help even if it meant getting her hands dirty. She may have had to scrub gummy handprints from her neck when she got home, but I believe the Lord saw them as a necklace of love and faithfulness. That certainly was true for one weary child and her exasperated mother in the supermarket check-out line.

Polish Your Jewels:

- What does Grandma Ethel show us about the significance of a simple act of human compassion?

- When were you recently the recipient of an undeserved kindness? How did it make you feel?

- What are some things you can do to reflect God's love and ease the lives of those around you?

- Make a list of ten loving things you can do for others, and then do one a week for the next ten weeks.

Day 2: Glistening

"Plans fail for lack of counsel, but with many counselors they succeed." (Prov 15:22)

....

Scripture Insight: As a counselor, asking for advice should come easily for me. Sadly, I often let pride, fear, or ignorance keep me from the help I need to accomplish a given task. Then, floundering in frustration, I realize how much I need the counsel of those who have gone before me. When it came to running a 10K, I learned that the hard way.

Want to Be Part of Our Team?

We had a saying in the South when I was growing up: "Southern girls don't sweat; they glisten." That was true even in physical education class, which I had to attend faithfully every seventh period, all through high school. Physical workouts were a chore for me, so you can imagine my surprise when I moved to California to attend college and met girls in the dorm who ran—for fun! They invited me to go with them, and what's even more surprising, I liked it. So there I was, running with my new friends every day, "glistening" all around the track and enjoying it.

I grew to love running so much that the habit stuck with me long after I graduated from college. I ran to relieve stress when I got my first real job. I ran to take off unwanted pounds after the birth of each of my three kids. I ran so that I wouldn't succumb to middle-age spread. But I had never run competitively until my friend Denise recruited me in my mid-thirties to run a 10K marathon with her. "You can do it, Linda. It's only six miles. Step up your daily distance and you'll be fine," she encouraged.

"Girl, I can't run six miles with a hound on my heels," I argued. But Denise was a tough cookie. She regularly ran in races and won most of them, and she wasn't going to listen to my excuses. So I began adding more "glisten time" to my schedule every day.

Our area was hilly and remote, so I was out on the road every day after work, putting one foot in front of the other. If I left work late, I found myself running in the dark, but I was determined to get my miles in.

Not long after I began training, my husband and I were on our way to do some grocery shopping when he turned into the sporting goods store. "Where are we going?" I asked.

"Well, if you're training for a marathon, you're going to need new shoes."

Bruce had shown little interest in my exercise regimen, so his comment took me by surprise. However, far be it from me to turn down new clothes of any kind. We spent an hour picking out the perfect shoes with proper arch support for my feet, and bought several pairs of expensive socks to go with them. Now I was out there every day with a vengeance, inspired by my comfortable new running shoes.

A couple of weeks later, Bruce walked into the kitchen where I was preparing dinner after my evening run. "I have a present for you," he grinned. It was a small box.

"Jewelry? What's the occasion?"

"Wait till you see," he responded, still grinning. Opening the box, I found a state-of-the-art runner's watch. This gadget took your pulse, timed your laps, and compared your times. Why, it did everything but jump out of bed and run for you! Now I was running every day in style with my new shoes and socks, plus my fancy runner's watch.

The day of the marathon came. I was up bright and early after carb-loading the night before. Denise and I had agreed to meet in the parking lot next to the registration booth, but when I arrived the lot was swarming with people. I searched for Denise in earnest, even checking the women's restroom. (*That's always a good meeting place*, I thought.) I asked several women who were engrossed in contorted warm-up stretches, but they barked at me as if I had asked for a kidney. By now I was feeling intimidated and defeated. A voice on the loudspeaker called for women who had entered the 10K.

I wasn't sure where the starting line was, so I lined up with a group of ladies who looked like they knew what they were doing. I leaned over my ankles like *Runners World* magazine said I should do, then I ran—straight to my car. I cried all the way home. I was angry at myself for giving up, frustrated that I had wasted all of that preparation time, and determined *never* to try this again.

Denise called later that day. She said she had arrived late and couldn't find me in the crowd either. She swore herself to secrecy about my meltdown, but I resolved that my racing days were over. Or so I thought.

Barely a year later, a group at our church was putting together a team to run the Sacramento Marathon to raise funds for a mission trip. "I hear that you run, Linda." The comment came from Kenny, a seasoned firefighter, on our way out of church one day. "Do you want to be part of our team?"

I told Kenny the whole story of my sorry day at the races. "It will be different this time, Linda," he said. "We work as a team. We'll train with you and support you. We won't let you get discouraged and run away. It will be great. What do you say?" With a pitch like that, I could not say anything but yes.

Kenny was true to his word. We did train as a team and helped each other with our weaknesses while praising each other's strengths. The day of the race came too soon. But when my time came, I tagged my partner and ran a six-mile leg of the 26.2-mile marathon. On my fifth mile, when I didn't know how I could finish, I heard cheers from the sidelines. My teammates who had already run and were exhausted had waded through the crowd for miles to encourage me.

I made it to the contact point with barely a breath left but with an incredible sense of accomplishment in my heart. After a short rest, we all headed for the finish line.

Screaming cheers of encouragement, we welcomed our last teammate across the line. We all felt the victory.

Standing there glistening in that huge crowd, I learned something vital: whether you're tackling the Sacramento Marathon or the marathon of life, the race is a lot easier when you run with teammates.

Polish Your Jewels:

- When was the last time you asked someone for insight or advice?

- Did that person give you advice in a palatable way?

- Did your experience inspire you to ask again, or did you retreat to safety and try to do things on your own?

- How do you give advice to your co-workers, friends, and family members?

Day 3: Experience

"Gray hair is a crown of splendor; it is attained by a righteous life." (Prov 16:31)

....

Scripture Insight: In a culture obsessed with youth and beauty, we're slow to recognize the wisdom that comes with age. The experiences of life can teach us a lot, especially when we walk each day with Christ. Even the tough times have something to impart to us.

The Message renders Hebrews 12:7 this way: "God is educating you; that's why you must never drop out. He's treating you as dear children." In the NIV, it goes on to say in verse 11: "No discipline seems pleasant at the time, but painful. Later on, however, it produces a harvest of righteousness and peace for those who have been trained by it."

We choose whether the circumstances of life will make us better or bitter.

Grace Short

Her name was Grace Short, but she should have been called Grace Long, because she certainly was long on grace. This gentle Southern lady in her seventies was my junior-high Sunday school teacher. Week after week, she came into our classroom with the patience of Job and the persistence of the apostle Paul. She needed both qualities to tackle our class of unruly adolescents.

My twin sister and I were new Christians. Not having been raised in a Christian home, we didn't know how to behave in church. My mom worked the night shift at a local restaurant, and when she left each evening, we ran wild in the neighborhood. No one could expect us to sit still for an hour of Sunday school. We were kids about whom proper Southern ladies with beads and beehives would say while sipping sweet tea , "Those young'uns just ain't had no raisin'!"

But that didn't scare Mrs. Short. She showed up each week with a lesson that she had clearly spent hours preparing. She shared scriptures, illustrations, and personal stories with us. To be honest, I came not only because I wanted to hear what she had to say but because I wanted to be with her. She was soft-spoken and gentle, like no one else in my life. Her white hair rested against wrinkled cheeks, and she always looked like the portrait of a perfect lady, complete with pearl necklace and matching earrings. She carried a lily-white hankie to dab her eyes, as she cried easily when she shared stories from God's Word that clearly meant so much to her. She got so excited talking about David's courage or Saul's transformation on the Damascus Road that she said she had "chill bumps." She always called me "Sugah" or "Darlin'." I felt I could trust her.

One Sunday morning after class, she asked me to wait for her. I had been asking questions all morning about Moses. ("Where did the Ten Commandments come from? Why did God pick Moses to lead his people? What was that 'plague' thing all about?") Mrs. Short asked me to follow her to the church library. We walked up stairs to a small room just off the main entrance lined floor-to-ceiling with books. After riffling through the dust-covered shelves, she pulled out a tattered paperback copy of *Good News for Modern Man* (TEV Bible) and handed it to me.

"I'm so sorry," she said with her sweet Southern drawl. "This is all I could find."

"Find for what?"

"To give to you, of course."

"You mean I get to keep this?" I asked, baffled by Mrs. Short's generosity.

"You asked so many questions that I thought you would enjoy reading the stories for yourself," she said with a broad smile.

"Yes, ma'am!"

On the walk home, I found myself in awe of the woman's kindness. *Why would she care this much about me?* I wondered.

I read fifty pages of my new Bible before our next Sunday school class session. I could not get enough of God's Word. The next Sunday, Mrs. Short told me that she wanted me to meet her on the church steps afterward. What could she have in store for me now? I was still in awe of the previous week's caring gesture as I headed to the church entrance after class. There I met Mr. Laxton, a tall, friendly retired pastor from the congregation who was our Sunday school superintendent.

"Grace told me how glad you were when she found a paperback Bible for you. I thought you would really enjoy this one," he said, handing me a red leather-bound Bible with my name engraved on the front.

I was too stunned to speak. Tears filled my eyes. "This is for me?"

"Has your name on the front," he chuckled. "You can thank Mrs. Short for that. She wanted to make sure you had a way to learn more about the Lord."

Now I was the one dabbing tears as Mrs. Short leaned over, hugged me, and said, "Don't it just give you chill bumps?"

I hadn't had many good role models to that point in my life, but now I wanted to be just like Grace Short, who was long on grace and full of God's love.

Polish Your Jewels:

- Have the experiences of life made you better or bitter? How might the bitter lessons make you better?

- Have hard times produced a "harvest of righteousness and peace" in your character? How?

- Define grace. How do you demonstrate grace in your relationships?

Day 4: Filled

"A miserable heart means a miserable life; a cheerful heart fills the day with song." (Prov 15:15 MSG)

Scripture Insight: My mother-in-law told me that *attitude* was mind over matter: "If you don't mind, it doesn't matter." Unfortunately, many of us mind our circumstances too much. We fret and worry, majoring on minors, chronically seeing the cup half empty instead of half full. We go through life playing our negative notes and wondering why no one wants to listen to our song.

An attitude of misery is always available, but so is an attitude of hope. Whether we are content in life depends on where we put our focus. When you find yourself plinking the negative note of "what's wrong with the world today," it's time to change your tune! In my book *Twelve Ways to Turn Your Pain into Praise*, I recommend the Faithful Fifteen to change your negative attitude: Make a copious list of your blessings; then devote fifteen minutes each day to reading and rereading your list. Fill your heart with an awareness of blessing and your heart will fill the day with song.

What's in Your Cup?

Jacob was born the middle child of our family and my only son. Despite having two devoted parents and two sisters who adored him, he had an uncanny knack for seeing the cup of life as half empty.

Every day after school, Jake would slouch through the door, fall on his bed, and begin a litany of everything bad that had happened that day. Despite my best efforts, he could not be dissuaded from his daily downward spiral.

On his ninth birthday, we saved enough money to take him to Disneyland for two whole days. (That's no easy feat on a pastor's salary!) After doing Disneyland to death, we collapsed in our hotel room and I asked, "Did you have fun today, Jake?"

He said, "Pirates of the Caribbean was closed!"

"Jacob, we stood in line for an hour and a half to see the Haunted Mansion. We rode Space Mountain three times. We walked in the park for two solid days, and all you can say is, 'Pirates of the Caribbean was closed'?" I was unable to contain my exasperation. Clearly, something had to be done about his negative attitude.

Lord, please help me help this child, I prayed as I drifted off to sleep.

On my next trip to the bookstore, I found what I was looking for. It was a book by Florence Littauer titled *Your Personality Tree,* which describes how parents can positively shape the personalities of their children. From the description in the book, Jake appeared to be a melancholy child: he was sensitive, artistic, deep, analytical, and able to see the worst in every situation.

Littauer had a fascinating suggestion for shifting his paradigm. Since melancholics have an emotional need for order and sensitivity, she suggested that I listen to all the woes he saw in his world. My usual reaction was to try to talk Jake out of his negativity, but that wouldn't satisfy his need for sensitivity. I had to let him finish his lament and ask, "What *good* things happened today?" Then I needed to wait until he could tell me—wait for as long as it took. This would help Jake realize that good things really were happening to him despite his woeful perspective.

Armed with this idea, I determined to shift his negative paradigm if it killed us both! Jake came home from school, flopped down on his bed as usual (consistent behavior is an attribute of the melancholy personality), and again began to tick off his list of the terrible things that had happened at school. I listened attentively, making eye contact and nodding with empathy before I asked, "What good things happened today, Jake?"

His response was, "Nothing."

"Something good had to happen. You were there all day," I encouraged. Then I waited. I waited fifteen long minutes that first day, determined to stay there all night if that's what it took to break his pattern of pessimism.

At last he admitted, "I did get to dust the erasers."

"By yourself?"

"No, with Brandon."

"Your best bud?"

"Yeah."

"You mean you got to leave class and dust erasers with your best friend? You're one lucky kid, if you ask me!"

"Yeah, I guess I am," Jake remarked with his head back and his shoulders squared.

This began a daily ritual for us. Then at age nineteen, Jake was off to college on a music scholarship. He hadn't been there for more than three weeks when I got a call. "Mom, they're killing me here! I go to classes all morning, music practice in the afternoon, and drama rehearsal until midnight. Then I get up and do it all again the next day!" he moaned.

"I know, Jake, but you get to pay for your education by doing what you love. Your buddy Mark has to hang drywall to pay for his education."

"But Mom," he continued, "they're *killing* me!"

I quickly interrupted. "Jacob," was all I got out. I used a tone he had learned well in all those years of debriefing. "I know, I know, Mom," he said. "What's full in the cup?" Then he began listing things that were good about his situation.

Today, my son is an amazing musician. But when he begins to spiral downward, as his temperament predisposes him to do, he has learned to focus on what's full in his cup. As a wonderfully artistic, sensitive, introspective songwriter, he has discovered that "a miserable heart makes a miserable life; a cheerful heart fills the day with song."

Polish Your Jewels:

- What's full in the cup of your life? Make a list. Post it on your mirror, computer screensaver, and refrigerator door. Pause to thank God for your blessings every time you look at the list.

- Do you notice a difference in your attitude as you focus on your blessings?

- Make a conscious decision to consider the good in each situation before you complain. Read Romans 8:28: "And we know that in all things God works for the good of those who love him, who have been called according to his purpose."

Day 5: Plans

"We can make our plans, but the Lord determines our steps." (Prov 16:9 NLT)

....

Scripture Insight: Have you ever planned things perfectly, only to encounter an interruption that provided the most perfect plan of all? Have you ever experienced a divine detour that was frustrating at first but proved to be fabulously fulfilling in the end? (Ever been annoyed when writers use alliteration to make memorable points?)

When we follow God, our road isn't predictable. I guess that's why it's called a "faith walk." I've been on that road long enough to learn how to look for life's lessons rather than snivel about its setbacks. On this trip, we need to strap in for a wild ride!

The "Magic" Magic Mountain Trip

I guess you've heard that I'm leaving," Matt said as we left a staff meeting at church.

"I heard, and we are really going to miss you. So are the kids." Matt had been a real godsend to the kids in our youth group. He was good-looking, God-loving, smart, funny, and totally cool. He was everything a high-school kid hoped to find in a youth pastor.

"I don't want to see all of my hard work go down the tubes," Matt continued as we walked down the hall. "The kids need someone to take my place, and every time I pray, the Lord makes clear that it's you, Linda."

"I don't know which God you've been talking to," I protested. "I have three teenagers of my own, and even they don't like me most of the time. Now you want me to lead a room full of them? You don't seem to understand. I'm terminally uncool. I was uncool even when I was in high school myself. I was the kid with her head in a book all the time."

But Matt was compelling and so was the Lord. I finally said yes.

I had been youth pastor for a few short months when I received a brochure in the mail announcing that the Magic Mountain amusement park was having a Christian Music Day. Matt had relocated to that area, so he called and suggested that I bring our group down. Our worship band could play a concert, the kids could see their former youth pastor, and both youth groups could hang out at Magic Mountain.

The plan sounded good, but I felt the magnitude of transporting a group of high school kids to Los Angeles, traveling the freeways on a church bus. Kids did some pretty dumb things on buses when I was in high school. I was apprehensive, so I prayed hard.

Kenny Jordan, a fireman and awesome youth worker, agreed to drive our bus. We met on Friday afternoon at the high school, loaded up, and set off. About an hour down the road, Kenny noticed smoke pouring from the back of the bus. He pulled over and so did Peter Bower, who was following us in a van carrying the music equipment and a few kids who couldn't fit on the bus. Peter was a master mechanic and I found myself thanking God we had him with us. After a bit of tinkering, he had us on the road again.

About halfway to LA, a car pulled up beside us, honking its horn. The driver was yelling and pointing to the right side of the bus. It was on fire! We quickly pulled over again and I quickly ushered the kids off the bus. Kenny and Peter slid under the bus. (If your bus catches on fire, it's nice to be traveling with a master mechanic and a fireman!) They put out the fire and soon found the cause: The transmission was leaking oil from the flywheel onto the exhaust manifold. I didn't understand what they were saying; I just knew I had thirty-five kids on the side of a freeway in the middle of farm country. I struggled to think of options.

As I walked around the bus to check on our group, I couldn't believe my eyes. The kids were huddled in a circle, heads bowed, praying! They had no concern about missing the fun at Magic Mountain. They were asking God's protection for Peter and Kenny. They were praying for wisdom for me. And I heard a few simple prayers of, "Help, Lord!"

Just then, a family pulled up in an old van. A tall, slender man walked over. Speaking in broken English, he said, "I saw the bus and the kids praying. I wanted to see if I could help. I'm a Christian. My name is Hey-sus." Looking at the name on his blue mechanic's shirt, I read *Jesus*! (How about that? Our youth group prayed for help and Jesus showed up!) We all introduced ourselves to the Good Samaritan and he asked again, "Is there anything I can do to help?"

"I don't think so," Peter replied. "It's a fairly complicated transmission problem and the bus is old…"

Jesus broke into a big smile. "I have a transmission shop. It's just down the road in Pixley. We can take your bus there to fix it. You all must stay at my house. It is a big house with much room. My family will welcome you. We will feed the children. It will be a great blessing for us."

We looked at each other. I thought, *We don't know this guy from Adam. Can I trust him with these kids?* I cast a questioning glance at Pete, who was a part-time deputy sheriff. I figured that if Pete thought the man could be trusted, I would trust his judgment.

"God bless you, brother," Pete said, pumping Jesus's hand.

"I have a friend from church who owns a pizza parlor," Jesus continued. "I will call him. I'm sure he will feed you all."

All I could muster was, "OK. We're all hungry."

Peter grabbed a piece of scrap metal from the side of the road. With an old piece of wire, he and Kenny mounted it under the carriage to prevent oil from dripping onto the hot manifold until we could get to Pixley.

When we pulled into the tiny pizza place, the lights were still on. We walked in to find piping hot pizzas everywhere.

We ate our fill, and I had to convince the dear owner to take payment for what we had eaten.

After piling back onto the bus, we drove to Jesus's 950-square-foot house. Jesus met us in the front yard. "Come inside, my friends," he said. It was very obvious he was proud of his home.

Everything inside was clean and tidy. He introduced his children, guitars came out, and we had an amazing time of worship right there in that little living room. I noticed Peter in one corner having a serious conversation with Jesus, who looked down and finally nodded. "Everyone listen up," Pete called out. "Jesus would like to share his testimony with us."

Our host spoke in a quiet, restrained voice. "I am originally from Puerto Rico, and I led a very bad life there. I was addicted to heroin for much of it. Heroin is more powerful than anything I had ever known. It led me to other things, and I ended up in prison for two years. After getting out, I went back to my old ways and was sent to prison again.

"One day as I was sitting in my cell so very sick and wondering where my next 'fix' would come from, I wondered how I had gotten this way. I cried out to Jesus and asked him to take the addiction away. I told him I was sorry and that I needed him to be my Savior. A wonderful peace came over me and I fell asleep. When I woke up the next morning, I had no desire for the drug and never did after that. When I was released from prison, I met my wife Maria and we moved here. God has blessed us with children, this fine home, and a business to support us. Thank you for listening to me." With that, Jesus humbly sat down.

You could have heard a pin drop as the young audience absorbed what he had said. Jesus's testimony broke open prayerful conversations all over the room. Kenny, Pete, and I counseled with kids long into the night.

The next morning, we loaded our young people onto the bus and headed for a city park across the street from Jesus's transmission shop. As soon as they got off the bus, the kids formed a circle without my prompting and asked for God's wisdom, safety, and help. I felt so proud and blessed to be a part of their lives.

I walked into the garage, where Peter and Jesus were discussing what they needed to repair our old bus. I told our host how God had used his powerful life story to minister to our young people. "I'll bet you've shared that story at a lot of churches and youth gatherings," I ventured.

"Actually, that was the first time I have shared it," Jesus said.

"Well, it won't be the last."

The two men crawled under the bus and I heard Pete say, "Hey, I think I see our problem. This bolt worked its way loose and was lodged underneath the flywheel. That must have caused the leak."

Since I was no good with engine repair, I joined the kids in the park. As I sat talking with a group of girls, Pete began yelling from across the street. "You're not going to believe this!" he shouted. His grease-covered fingers held a bolt. "This is the part we need to fix our bus. We thought we'd have to special-order it, but I walked over to this big bucket of spare parts in the corner of Jesus's garage. There I found this bolt—the very one we needed—resting on top of the pile. We'll be on the road in fifteen minutes!"

We gathered the youth group and told them the amazing story. To show our appreciation for all his kindness, we asked Jesus if we could take his fifteen-year-old son with us to Magic Mountain. "Of course," he replied. No one in his family had ever visited an amusement park.

We had a great time at Magic Mountain, but the rest of the day paled in comparison to what had already happened. We still call it our "*Magic* Magic Mountain Trip."

Polish Your Jewels:

- Describe a divine detour in your life. What did you learn from that experience?

- Has God ever asked you to move out of your comfort zone to serve him?

- When you did that, what did you learn about yourself? About God?

Day 6: Wholehearted

"Let your eyes look straight ahead, fix your gaze directly before you. Make level paths for your feet and take only ways that are firm. Do not swerve to the right or the left; keep your foot from evil." (Prov 4:25–27)

....

Scripture Insight: I have gleaned wisdom for living from a unique source, my dog. Here are just a few things I've learned from my faithful mutt, Gus: Don't bite the hand that feeds you. A good run will always make you feel better. Be loyal to those around you and they will return the favor. Last but not least, if you're going to do something, give it all you've got. Whether it's patrolling the perimeter or barking it up on the porch, Gus commits himself wholeheartedly to the task at hand.

Good Ol' Gus

I remember the summer day I first met Gus. I opened the screen door to feed our feeble terrier, Lacey, when a large ball of energy with tufts of red-brown fur accosted me.

"Look who followed me home," my husband Bruce said as he came up the driveway from his morning walk. He pointed to the overgrown puppy, whose panting face made it appear as though he was smiling ear to ear. "He was wandering in front of the house this morning, and he followed me the entire time I walked. I bet he's hungry."

"If he wasn't a pup, he'd be scary looking, with all that red fur and those strange green eyes," I remarked.

"Still, he's got to be thirsty after walking for two miles," Bruce persisted.

"You know that if we feed him, he's going to stick around. We already have Lacey. Do we really need another dog to care for?"

"I'm not sure we have a choice. I think he wants us!"

I brought out another bowl and the stray puppy ate like there was no tomorrow.

"Poor thing, he *is* hungry," Bruce remarked.

"We'll see who you're calling 'poor' when the kids wake up. If they lay eyes on him, they'll beg us to let him stay. He's a big dog. Can we afford to feed him?" Money was tight, and some months I wondered how we would feed the kids, much less another pet.

I was right. As soon as my younger daughter, Ashley, spotted the dog on the front porch, all I heard was, "Please, Mom, can he stay? Let us keep him, please! We'll call him Gus." (She named him after the enthusiastic mouse Gus-Gus, from Disney's *Cinderella*.) When the other two kids woke up, they played and laughed with their energetic new friend all day.

Realizing I was outvoted, that evening I informed my kids that if we were going to keep Gus, we needed to clean him up. Since we knew nothing about where he came from, I wasn't willing to bathe him in our bathtub, where we washed Lacey in comfortable warm water. "You'll have to bathe Gus outside and use the hose," I announced.

Ashley and her brother Jake wrestled Gus into submission as we hosed him with cold water and suds. By the time of the final rinse, I was sold. Any dog that would put up with that ordeal must really want a home. "OK," I conceded. "Gus is ours."

"Yay!" they cheered. Gus jumped and barked too, as if he knew exactly what I had said.

Not long after our new pet joined the family, we moved into a trailer on a remote six-acre parcel while we built a new house. One morning as Ashley opened the door to step out, Gus began growling and barking. I rushed to the door and spotted a rattlesnake right where Ashley would have stepped. Gus had seen it first and warned his girl as best he could.

Late one evening in the construction process, my older daughter Sarah pulled into the driveway and saw a drama unfold from her car window. Apparently, our arthritic dog Lacey had fallen into a trench that had been dug for the septic tank and was unable to get out. Sarah watched as Gus moved in behind Lacey and gently nudged her to safety.

But Jake had the honor of being the family member with whom Gus would "talk." Gus adopted our family just as Jake was moving into the angst of adolescence. Often as he lay on his bed, troubled by the current state of his junior-high world, Gus would enter the room, settle beside his bed, and growl in low, hushed phrases that resembled sentences of comfort and encouragement to his boy.

One Thanksgiving when Gus had matured, I commented during a family discussion that Gus had shown up out of nowhere, like an angel, and had watched over us ever since. Shaun, Sarah's husband, laughed and asked, "So you think Gus just showed up on your doorstep that day?"

"Shaun, what do you know?" my husband asked.

"Sarah spotted Gus wandering the streets by the high school and brought him home. She left him in the front yard because she knew you'd all fall in love with him." Sarah admitted it was true.

Gus may have found a home that day, but we were blessed with a great example of perseverance and loyalty. Now I strive to be half as faithful as my dog—and half as good as he thinks I am!

Polish Your Jewels:

- Do you find it hard to "let your eyes look straight ahead" and "fix your gaze directly before you" in your daily Christian walk?

- How can you "make level paths for your feet and take only ways that are firm"?

- Do you ever wish you could be as loyal and wholehearted as your dog? What simple steps could you take today?

Day 7: The Gift

"Never walk away from someone who deserves help;
your hand is God's hand for that person."
(Prov 3:27 MSG)

....

Scripture Insight: If the greatest gift we can offer someone is
the opportunity to know Jesus Christ, why is it so difficult
to share our faith? If we Christians believe what the Bible
says about hell and eternal punishment, why do we hesitate
to tell anyone about God's saving grace?

Is this a matter of such great consequence that we're
afraid of doing it wrong? Do we hesitate to mention
salvation because it might be controversial? Or have we
adopted an attitude of universal tolerance, forgetting that
Jesus said, "I am the way and the truth and the life. No one
comes to the Father except through me" (John 14:6)?

Without Christ, a person is condemned for all eternity.
I couldn't let that happen to my dad, so I offered him the
greatest gift I had.

Divots and Divine Encounter

I was ready to go back to college when I felt a nudge
from the Lord one morning to have a heart-to-heart
talk with my dad. With only two days before my flight,
I didn't know how that would happen. Then the phone
rang. "Hey, Lin. Can you come play nine holes with me?"
dad asked.

"Sure, daddy!" *Thank you, Lord*, I whispered under my breath.

I've never been a good golfer. I'm convinced that every course I play has to call a special repair crew for all the divots I create. That day was no exception, because my head was not in the game. I had something more important on my mind: my father's eternal soul.

When we arrived at the ninth hole, I pulled out my putter and poured out my heart. "Daddy, I need to talk with you."

"What is it, Doll?" he asked, smacking his ball into the hole without looking up. My dad's skill was amazing.

"Daddy, I've been gypped," I said, my words punctuated with sobs. "I haven't had you around for so many years and I've really missed out. I want to make sure you'll be around forever."

"Slow down, Honey," Dad pleaded. "I can barely understand you."

I breathed a prayer for peace and the words continued to flow: "Daddy, all of your daughters including me are going to heaven, and we want you to be there with us. The only way for that to happen is for you to accept Jesus as your Savior. I have to go back to California soon, and I'll worry about you the entire time I'm gone until I know you're OK with God."

"I know, Doll," Dad said, "and I'm going to do something about that."

"You do? You are?"

"Yes."

Immediately, I thought, *Let's do something right now.* But I felt a check from the Lord, so we talked no more about it. We finished our golf game, I hugged my dad good-bye, and he headed back to work while I set off for the pastor's office.

The pastor's wife was at the receptionist's desk. Phyllis was a sweet, soft-spoken lady with a heart full of compassion. I told her about the conversation that had just taken place on the golf course. "My daddy is so ready," I said. "I just know that if Pastor Gales talked with him, he would give his heart to the Lord."

"Don't you worry, Honey. I'll tell him everything you said."

Three weeks after the semester began, my sister and I received a letter from home. My stepmother was good at keeping us updated on family news. "Your little sister is taking scuba-diving lessons," she wrote. "The Mr. Lincoln roses are blooming beautifully. And by the way, the pastor came to visit and your dad and I gave our hearts to Christ."

She stated it so matter-of-factly that I read it over several times before the reality sank in. When it finally did, Bev and I began yelling the good news to perfect strangers all over campus: "Our folks accepted Christ!" There could not have been a better place to get this news than on a Christian college campus. People we didn't know were hugging us and crying. They were excited about our parents' newfound faith, and we were overjoyed!

My dad had offered us a safe place away from our mother's abuse. Now he had a safe place for eternity, and we will be together forever. If they have golf courses in heaven, you'll find us on the back nine.

Polish Your Jewels:

- Is Christ prompting you to talk with someone about him? Remember, if he's prompting you, he's preparing them.

- Ask others to pray for you to overcome your fear and do it. Then pray for the other person's heart to remain open.

- If you don't have a burden for an unsaved friend or family member, ask God to give you one.

Day 8: Light

"The path of the righteous is like the first gleam of dawn, shining ever brighter till the full light of day." (Prov 4:18)

....

Scripture Insight: I want to be a light for people who are stumbling in the darkness, but it's not easy. I must get out of the way by surrendering to Christ's power daily.

As Christians, we pray for others to see God in us. The more we know him, the brighter his love will shine through us. Francis of Assisi said, "Preach the gospel at all times, and if necessary, use words."

The School of Fish

Scripture says that older Christian women should teach younger ones, but many times the older we get, the crankier we become and no one wants to hang around us—least of all young people! Have you ever approached an older lady with an innocent, "How are you?," only to get a catalog of aches, pains, and problems?

I was blessed with a rare gem named Edith Fish. Edith was an older lady in our Sierra Pines church who made everyone feel like the most significant person on the planet. The minute you said hello, she would lavish love on you, ask with sincere interest about your family, and end the conversation with some empowering word of encouragement.

"Your kids are lucky to have you as their mother," she would say. Or, "Teenagers are tough, but you're doing a great job." Or, "Dear, you've planned a delightful tea. Everything is lovely, thanks to you." Edith wasn't the old lady everyone tried to avoid. She was the belle of the ball wherever she went.

In the early days of our congregation, our women's group was small enough to meet in various ladies' homes. When Edith shared her experiences, women would literally sit on the floor by her feet and listen to her loving wisdom. After a while, she would say, "I'm sure you don't want to listen to the meanderings of an old woman."

But we would protest, "No, Edith. Please tell us more!"

She told us about raising five kids on a shoestring budget. Edith shared her life story with honesty and authenticity. There was no vain pride or smug spirituality, just a real-life Christian mother's story with a touch of humor, which was exactly what we young mothers needed.

We laughed till we cried as she told about the morning when she was pregnant with child number four, her youngest was in a high chair, and the oldest had left the breakfast table screaming, "The washer is running over!" At that moment, just as her two-year-old dumped a cup of orange juice into Edith's front pocket, someone knocked on the door! We had all been in situations like that, and it was reassuring to hear another mother's story.

Edith made God look good. As a young mother, I concluded that I wanted to be Edith when I grew up. I enrolled in the "School of Fish," listening to Edith's insight every chance I got. I tried to model her patience with children and her devotion to her family. I purposed in my heart to remain genuine and honest, even in my older years. I didn't want the light of my joy to grow dim with complaining. I continue to pray for it to shine brighter with each passing year, just like my friend Edith Fish.

Polish Your Jewels:

- Ask the Lord to illuminate the places where you need to look more like him.

- Surrender your self-absorbed attitude to the Lord.

- Pray daily for God's life-transforming power.

- Find spiritual mentors to model your life after.

Day 9: Fear

"Those who fear the Lord are secure; he will be a place of refuge for their children." (Prov 14:26 NLT)

....

Scripture Insight: Growing up in a home filled with anger and violence, I learned early to associate the word *fear* with danger and dread. So when I read in the Bible that I was supposed to fear God, my mind conjured up images of a Dirty Harry in the sky, hovering over the "smite" button on the console of heaven, just waiting for me to mess up.

The Hebrew word for *fear* in this verse does not mean to cower in terror. It means to reverence or treat with deep devotion and respect. *Vine's Bible Dictionary* describes it as a "reverential fear of God, a controlling motive of life, in matters spiritual and moral. It is…a wholesome concern for displeasing Him." Ironically, this kind of reverence or awe banishes the fear that would otherwise cause us to shrink from God's presence.

The apostle Paul further explains this in Romans 8:15–16: "For you did not receive a spirit that makes you a slave again to fear, but you received the Spirit of sonship. And by him we cry 'Abba, Father.' The Spirit himself testifies with our spirit that we are God's children." God's Word tells us not to be debilitated by fear but to embrace God's love like that of a father—specifically, the love of "Abba," which is translated as "Daddy."

Ask Your Daddy

It was one of those rare summer days in central California when the sky darkens and the air smells like rain. Ashley Rose, my five-year-old daughter, was playing outside with the little neighbor girl, Jessie. Those two could play together for hours, but with the clouds coming up, I worried that lightning might soon follow. I decided to call the girls inside.

As I approached the front door, their conversation caught me off guard. They spoke in low, hushed tones that signified a deep, meaningful discussion, uncharacteristic of kindergarten girls. Jessie tearfully said, "I have to have surgery on my foot, and I'm scared!"

I watched as Ashley wrapped her arm around her playmate and patted her back. She knew all too well what Jessie had to fear. Ashley Rose had already survived two heart surgeries and was awaiting a more serious open-heart surgery in just a few months.

Ashley made it a habit to squirm into our bed every evening. She would cuddle up between her dad and me and then pose question after question: "Is it going to hurt like it did last time?" "Can Sissy and Jake come and see me?" "Will they let me keep Bobo [her teddy bear] with me?"

Her daddy patiently answered her questions, even as her doubts became more personal: "Why am I like this but Jake and Sarah aren't?" "Will I always be this small?" "Am I going to die?" However long it took each night, her daddy was willing to devote time to his special child.

So it came to no surprise to me that, as she sat with her arm around Jessie, she said confidently, "You don't have to worry. Just talk to your daddy." Ashley knew that her daddy would be there to help her, offering comfort and peace.

Our God, Abba-Father, our Daddy, longs to do the same for us if we will allow him. How long has it been since you confided to him your doubts and fears? He's waiting, and he's got all the time in the universe for you.

Polish Your Jewels:

- Have you ever felt engulfed by the Lord's love, sensing comfort that brought you great peace? Capture those feelings in a journal and refer to them often, especially when your faith is weak.

- What prevents you from trusting God to help you? Is it insecurity, fearing that you aren't worthy of his help? Do you suspect he is not willing to help you?

- Lay those obstacles at Christ's feet in prayer, trusting him to be there for you. If you can't get past these obstacles, talk with another Christian about what you are feeling.

Day 10: Words

"The right word at the right time is like a custom-made piece of jewelry." (Prov 25:11 MSG)

....

Scripture Insight: One of my greatest desires is to bring joy to people by saying the right word at the right time. I want God's love to shine through me, so I pray that my words will speak healing to those God brings across my path. And he often arranges for others to return the favor.

Nancy's Note

One of the best parts of my ministry is working with women at retreats. Whether I'm speaking to a group or counseling one-on-one, I feel God's power and presence during those weekends that are devoted to him. That was true the weekend I met Nancy.

The retreat had been planned for well over a year. It would offer activities that required hours of meticulous planning. In order to attend, a lady had to be sponsored by someone else. We wanted all of the women to feel God's attentive love as they experienced the care that went into this well-organized weekend.

The plan seemed to be working for everyone but Nancy. She was edgy and distant, even uncooperative. When it was time for a group activity, she sat alone. When we announced it was time to change activities, she became temperamental. After the first day of the event, our leaders met to debrief and assess how the women were responding. Nancy's name came up.

"I'm afraid she'll miss out on all the amazing revelations that God could have for her this weekend," Janie commented.

Susan chimed in. "Valerie worked so hard on her sponsorship. She even got Nancy's husband to write a letter that she will give her while she's here. I don't want either Nancy or Valerie to miss the blessings this weekend has to offer."

"Linda, will you talk to Nancy?" the event coordinator asked.

"I'll try," I replied, "but she doesn't seem to be responding to anyone. So you pray, and I'll do my part."

As the women were being ushered toward a generous snack table, I tapped Nancy on the shoulder. "Got a minute?" I asked, beckoning her to follow me. As we walked toward a quiet spot on the church campus, I said, "How's it going? Are you enjoying the retreat?"

"Is it that obvious?" Nancy responded. "I told my sponsor I really didn't want to be here, but she has counted on my attending this weekend for eight months. If I didn't think it would crush her, I'd walk away right now. I'm not in the mood to listen to a bunch of inspirational speakers. This has been the toughest week of my life."

"What happened?" I asked, patting the chair beside me. That's all it took. With a flood of tears, Nancy described events that would have wrecked a weaker woman.

"My husband Kal and I run a foster home for four at-risk adolescent boys. Last weekend he attended the men's version of this retreat, so I had all four boys by myself. They're a handful. I was looking forward to Monday so I could catch my breath. But on Sunday afternoon, my sister called and told me that her thirty-eight-year-old husband had committed suicide.

"My sister Karen is an emotional wreck," Nancy continued. "They have two boys, twelve and fourteen. So the minute Kal walked in the door, I drove four hours north. Karen could barely keep it together, so I had to handle the funeral arrangements and manage the boys. One minute they were crying inconsolably and the next they were acting out."

I nodded. Those grief reactions could be expected from kids that age. "You must be exhausted," I said.

"I am. The funeral was Thursday. Karen wanted it done quickly to get closure for herself and her boys. I got home just in time to come here."

"You were there for your sister. Who was there for you?" I asked.

"Kal would have been, but he had to care for our boys. So it's just been God and me dealing with this. I don't know about him, but I'm drained." She laughed and cried at the same time.

"I'm glad you haven't lost your sense of humor. I probably would have by now. Nancy, I think the events of this weekend could be just what you need. It's about so much more than just hearing other ladies teach from the Bible. But if I tell you what's to come, it will ruin some surprises your sponsor has worked so hard to prepare. I have a prayer exercise to suggest. I think it will help you dump some of your grief and stress so you'll be ready to receive all God has for you this weekend."

"Won't the leaders be frustrated if I'm not with the group? I know they already think I'm uncooperative."

"Let's let them go on to the next activity. We'll have our own retreat right here—you, me, and Jesus. What do you say?"

"I'm in," Nancy said, with the first smile I had seen from her all weekend.

We went through the prayer exercise.[1] When we were done, a look of relief came over her. The edgy lady was gone and a caring Christian sister had emerged. She prayed for me and the rest of the ladies on the retreat. We took turns praying for her sister and the boys. Time seemed to stand still as we lingered in the Lord's presence. Over an hour later, we returned to the group. Nancy joined in. She listened, laughed, and learned with the other women. Later that day, she thanked me for taking the time to pray with her.

"It was my pleasure," I said, hugging her.

The week after the retreat, I sent Nancy a card to let her know I was still praying for her. It had a picture of a lamb

---

1. Linda Newton, *Twelve Ways to Turn Your Pain into Praise* (Anderson, IN: Warner Press, 2008), 27–33.

resting serenely in the arms of Jesus. The artist made clear that the Lord was so attentive to the creature he's cradling that it could relax in utter repose. Inside, I wrote Jeremiah 29:11: "'For I know the plans that I have for you,' says the Lord. 'They are plans for good and not for disaster, to give you a future and a hope.'" I signed it, "Praying for you—Linda."

Two years passed. I was living in a twenty-foot travel trailer with my husband and three teenagers, two dogs, and a cat. We were building a new home on six acres at the end of the world. In order to save money, we had moved to the property with no phone and no power except a generator that I had to pull-start every day in the pouring rain of an El Niño winter.

My twelve-year-old daughter, Ashley, needed to have emergency heart surgery. We literally would have to live in UCLA's cardiac unit for a couple of weeks. As I stopped at the post office to pick up our mail, I noticed an envelope with Nancy's return address. Opening it, I found the very card that I had sent her. She had crossed through her name and wrote my name instead. There was a note at the bottom saying, "I don't know what's going on in your life right now, but you have been heavy on my mind. I felt led to pray for you and send this card back to you."

She could not have known all that I was experiencing, but our Lord did. *Lord, you really do have my back. Thank you for summoning Christian friends when I need them most.*

Polish Your Jewels:

- Does something have you feeling overwhelmed and hopeless? Cast that burden at the feet of Jesus (1 Pet 5:7).

- Have you ever felt a divine nudge to pray for someone? Take the time to respond, and let that person know you cared enough to do it.

Day 11: Reconciliation

"Gold there is, and rubies in abundance, but lips that speak knowledge are a rare jewel." (Prov 20:15)

....

Scripture Insight: I have received so much help by listening to the wise words of people whom God has placed on my path. Whether it's a pastor in the pulpit, a counselor on the radio, or a trusted friend on the telephone, these people care enough to listen to God and share that knowledge with others, including me. So it was that two women prepared me for a day of reconciliation that I didn't even know I needed.

Solid-Gold Friends

"Linda, I'm driving to a doctor's appointment and I feel the Lord prompted me to pray for you." Danise's sweet voice captured me as I listened to the voicemail on my office phone. "I have been praying for peace and strength for you—and for reconciliation." Danise was a faithful prayer warrior and a good friend. I could tell she was thoughtfully considering everything she had to say.

Tears welled up in my eyes. My schedule had been crazy. I was speaking every weekend at retreats and conferences while maintaining a full counseling load. I felt up to my eyeballs in projects at our local church that needed attention. In times like this, I often said to the Lord, "I love doing all that I do, just not all at the same time!" Danise's message reassured me that the Lord was calling on others to pray for the help I needed.

I felt Danise had accurately identified my first two needs, but I was puzzled by her last comment. What did I need to reconcile? I got no clear insight from the Lord about this, but I plowed through my busy week, feeling empowered as a result of her prayers.

As I sat in the Denver airport, my cell phone rang. It was my husband Bruce. "Sarah has her commissioning ceremony for the air force on Monday, and she wants us to go," he said.

I was stunned. Our oldest daughter Sarah was fiercely independent. At twenty-eight years old, in the middle of her doctoral studies in psychology, she had decided that she wanted to help soldiers returning from Iraq with post-traumatic stress disorder. Her husband Shaun was all for it. Shaun had served terms in Iraq just before he became an EMT. He was even considering reenlisting to join his wife in the air force. *I'm glad he's supportive, but I'm not convinced that my daughter will be all right in the military while our country is at war!* I'd said to myself again and again. "I thought… I thought they weren't taking her until next fall," I stammered into the cell phone.

"They aren't, but they're swearing her in right away. She wants us to be there. We'll have to leave early Monday morning. It's a four-hour drive to Sacramento. Will you be up for it after traveling all weekend?" Bruce asked.

"I wouldn't miss it," I replied.

As I sat reviewing my notes in the airport, my thoughts turned toward Sarah. Where would she be stationed? She had assured us that her work would keep her out of harm's way, but I knew our daughter. She was the little girl on the swing set always yelling, "Push me higher, Mommy!" She would volunteer for hazard duty. I was concerned about *her* stress level too, while dealing with so much post-traumatic stress in others. I hadn't shared these concerns with her because I never wanted to be a meddling mother. If she believed the Lord wanted her to help soldiers, who was I to get in her way?

I'm her mother, that's who! I thought. It became very clear in that moment that I was not happy with the idea of my petite, beautiful daughter becoming an officer in the United States Air Force during wartime. I had not reconciled myself to that idea.

Show me the path to reconciliation, Lord. I don't even know where to look for it, I honestly prayed.

"Now boarding for Tulsa," the loudspeaker announced.

The flight was brief and I found myself immediately busy with wonderful women in Sand Springs, Oklahoma. After my talk Saturday, I placed a chair in the middle of the room and invited women who needed prayer to come and sit in it while we gathered to pray for their needs. One by one, the ladies sat down and shared their hurts. After nearly three hours of praying, one of the women volunteered, "I think we should pray for Linda."

I immediately asked the group to pray for my daughter. "I have to confess that I am not crazy about her enlistment," I confessed. Ami, the senior pastor's wife, prayed that God would give me a sign that would calm my fears for Sarah. The prayers of other ladies offered much of that comfort. I arrived home late on Sunday evening, drained but delighted that God had blessed our weekend retreat.

Early the next morning, Bruce and I picked up Sarah and Shaun and headed for Sarah's commissioning ceremony. We arrived at what looked like a business office near a residential section of Sacramento. When every uniformed person in the building gathered to watch my daughter stand beside the American flag and be sworn in as a second lieutenant in the United States Air Force, I had to fight back the tears.

After lunch, we started for home. About an hour down the highway, we passed a green sedan driving on the shoulder. "Slow down and I'll get the license number and report it to the CHP," Shaun urged. We noticed that the driver, an older man, seemed unaware that he was driving illegally. He swerved back onto the highway and began weaving in and out of lanes. He clipped a white pick-up truck about four car-lengths ahead of us. We watched in what seemed to be a slow motion as the truck slammed against the guardrail, sending dust and vehicle parts flying everywhere.

We pulled to the side of the road as Bruce dialed 911. Then Sarah leaned forward, tapped her husband on the shoulder, and said, "Are we ready, Babe?"

I thought, *Ready? Ready for what?* But before I could ask that question, Sarah and Shaun had jumped out of our car and run into oncoming traffic. I watched my diminutive daughter's blond ponytail swinging in the wind as she flagged down an eighteen-wheeler to tell him about the accident ahead. I then jumped out of the car and followed her to the crushed pick-up.

There Shaun was already attending a three-year-old in the front seat with a cut on her cheek. "I need a cloth or something to put pressure on her wound," he called out.

I rushed back to our car to retrieve the stack of clean napkins that I had accumulated in my glove compartment. All the while, Sarah was calming the driver. Speaking half English and half Spanish, she asked the woman for her cell phone and then called the victim's brother to tell him where she was. By the time I returned with the napkins, a CHP desk officer from a station near the freeway had spotted the commotion and was on the scene. Clearly out of his element, he seemed to have no problem deferring to Sarah, who was giving everyone orders.

"Do you have a first-aid kit?" Sarah asked the officer. As he handed her the kit, she pointed to the driver of the green sedan. "You need to get that man's key," she said. "I think he might be deranged. He doesn't need to be on the road." The officer responded immediately.

Sarah dug through the first-aid kit, searching for items she needed to relieve the woman's pain. She kept assuring the victim that an ambulance would arrive soon.

I realized in that moment that I was absolutely useless except to pray, so I moved against the guardrail to get out of everyone's way. As I did, I sensed God saying, *Your daughter is not a little girl anymore, Linda. She is a grown woman capable of helping people. You have to let her go so she can do that.*

Danise's insight and Ami's prayer had prepared me for that moment of reconciliation. Standing in the median of a congested freeway, I thanked God that he was using my capable daughter. I also thanked him for sending me two women who helped me see that.

Polish Your Jewels:

- Have you ever tangibly felt that someone was praying for you? What did that do for your faith?

- When was the last time you prayed diligently for a friend?

- Make a list of several people God has used to bring truth into your life. Thank as many as you can for their contribution.

Day 12: Answers

"Hope deferred makes the heart sick, but a longing fulfilled is a tree of life." (Prov 13:12)

....

Scripture Insight: My childhood had been filled with so much pain that I thought I deserved a break in my adult years. So when my youngest daughter was born with life-threatening heart problems, I told the Lord I expected some answers. What I got instead was him; he was the answer.

Change of Heart

Ashley, my third child, came to us on a beautiful spring night in April. She was delivered by a midwife in our rural Oregon town. I was considered a low risk, having had two healthy children with normal deliveries. But nothing could have prepared me for what we were about to face with Ashley.

A routine check-up when Ashley was eleven days old ended in a five-hour trip to the nearest university hospital. A team of cardiologists met us there at nine o'clock that night. They whisked my baby away for an immediate examination.

After what seemed like an eternity, they brought back my weary, hungry child. Then a tall dark-haired doctor named Mary Rice stepped forward. With kind eyes and gentle voice, she soberly informed us, "Ashley has several complicated heart defects. She will need *many* surgeries in her life. We have her first emergency surgery scheduled for ten o'clock tomorrow morning."

In *The Message* paraphrase, Psalm 34:18 says, "If your heart is broken, you'll find God right there; if you're kicked in the gut, he'll help you catch your breath." I was kicked in the gut and God was holding me up. After many more tests, we finally settled down for the night, but I couldn't sleep. I couldn't eat. I couldn't even form a prayer. So my husband called our church in Oregon and my sister in North Carolina, and they graciously prayed for us. I envisioned a rainbow of prayer stretching from one end of the continent to the other for my precious Ashley.

The next morning, the nurses came to take my daughter for surgery. I watched as perfect strangers rolled my frightened baby away from me; I'd never felt so helpless in my life.

As I turned toward the waiting room, I caught a glimpse of the view from the seventh-floor hospital window. It was breathtaking, but I had been too preoccupied until now to notice. As I stood there, lost in the beauty of the lush green Oregon hillside, my eyes fell on a gorgeous garden spot. Caught up in the peaceful scene, I tried to pray. Then came the still small voice that I had been too overcome with confusion, grief, and fear to hear: *Ashley's not in the hands of strangers, Linda. She's in my hands.*

In my mind's eye, I could see Jesus amid the tall pines and azaleas. He was not alone. There sleeping serenely in his arms was my own precious Ashley Rose. As my eyes met his, I could hear him say, *There's room here for you, too, my child.*

Polish Your Jewels:

- Have you had a longing fulfilled? Remember how it made you feel. Thank God for his care.

- Is there a hope deferred in your life? Review what God has already done in your life. Trust him to continue his care.

Day 13: Learn

"Let the wise listen and add to their learning, and let the discerning get guidance." (Prov 1:5)

....

Scripture Insight: It has been said that if you stop growing, you'll start dying. Smart people continue to grow. They seek information and counsel. No matter how old we are, there is still something to learn. We need to position ourselves so we can do that.

The Blessed List

Earlene was poised and elegant as she made her way to the sofa in my office. In her late sixties, she spoke with confidence but with a twinge of anger in her voice. Her husband had recently retired and she was feeling the pressure of being with him 24/7. "He's driving me crazy!" she lamented. "I give him instructions on the simplest things, like making coffee or operating a blender, and then I end up repeating myself ten times before the task is completed. For goodness' sake, the man was an engineer for forty years! Have I spoiled him so badly that I've made him helpless? The truth is, no matter how much you love a guy, it's not easy to be around him all the time. I used to miss him while he was at work. Now I miss missing him!"

We both laughed, but I got her meaning. So I suggested she do two things. The first was to write a Blessed List.

That's a list of everything she loved and valued about her husband: everything he was or did that was a blessing to her. The second was to persuade her husband to see a doctor, just to make sure there was nothing wrong physically with him.

Two weeks later, she returned with a lengthy list of her husband's wonderful attributes. He was a good father and grandfather, he was an excellent provider, he was funny, and on and on. As she finished reading her list to me, she laid it on her lap and said, "I really have to thank you. Your gratitude exercise has changed my life. It made me realize what a great man I'm married to—even if he does drive me crazy at times."

"Keep reading your list," I encouraged. "Read it at least three times a day for the rest of the month, and then once a day after that. Add to it when you think of new things or when he does something that especially blesses you. The list can never get too long."

Earlene came to see me a couple more times. She was a quick study and she practiced what she was learning. I prayed that she would keep it up.

Three years passed and I received a letter with Earlene's name and Montana return address. She was living with her daughter. Three months after she came for counseling, she had convinced her husband to see a doctor, who discovered he had a brain tumor. He died five month later. "I am so grateful I had made a Blessed List," she wrote. "It changed my heart. I was reacting so negatively until I realized all the good my husband brought into my life. My paradigm shifted and I was able to love him as he ought to be loved before he died. Having an attitude of gratitude was a gift to him, but it was a gift to me as well, one I will never forget."

Despite her age and experience, Earlene didn't stop learning. She sought insight that changed her life for the better. We can all learn from her example.

Polish Your Jewels:

- Is there an area of your life where you feel spiritually or emotionally stuck? What have you done to gain the help you need?

- Is there a resource—such as a book, a Web site, a friend, or a counselor—that might help you? What prevents you from seeking that help?

- Pray for the Lord's help to move past any obstacles and avail yourself of the help you need.

Day 14: Firstfruits

"Honor the LORD with your wealth, with the firstfruits of all your crops; then your barns will be filled to over-flowing and your vats will brim over with new wine." (Prov 3:9–10)

....

Scripture Insight: I've never seen it to fail: When we honor God, he honors us. Today's scripture instructs us to give God our "firstfruits." Leviticus describes offering God the firstfruits of new corn (Lev 23:9–12). Numbers 28:26 talks about giving God the firstfruits of leavened bread. Exodus 34:26 instructs God's people to offer him the firstfruits of their soil.

I encourage you to offer God the firstfruits of your income. Pay God first. When you receive a paycheck, write a check for your tithe—10 percent of what you earn—and then watch how God provides the rest of what you need.

Being at the center of activity in a growing church, I've heard so many stories of how God provides for people when they make him their first priority. Stories like this one:

Peggy's Portion

Peggy was a hard-working woman. As a single mother with two children still at home, she had to be. Life had been difficult for a long time. After her parents divorced, Peggy had to grow up fast. Without much contact from her family, she paved life's path on her own.

Several failed marriages later, she walked through the doors at Sierra Pines church and instantly felt at home. "It was as if these people had known me my whole life," she told me. "They welcomed me with open arms. From the minute I walked in, I felt I was part of the family—and I really needed one.

"I joined a small group that had already been together for a year. Bill and Karen, the leaders, welcomed me into their home right away. Everyone in the group moved out of their comfort zone to embrace me. They included me in the weekly meetings, and they invited me to dinners and other outings they had."

Because the church had given so much to her, Peggy decided to give back by volunteering to serve as an usher and by plugging in wherever her busy schedule would allow. Her faith and friendships grew, which kept her spiritual tank filled, even when her employer fired four employees in five months, including her.

"I didn't know how God was going to provide, but I had a deep sense of peace that he would," Peggy confided. "So when I heard the church was sponsoring a couples retreat, I felt that Bill and Karen ought to go. With a house full of kids and only one income, a weekend retreat would be a luxury for them. They're like the parents I wish I'd had, the kind I want to be for my kids and grandkids."

She told me how she planned to surprise her small-group leaders. "Parents like them are always sacrificing for their children, so I felt God wanted them to have a turn. Linda, I'm giving you $100 today as a deposit for the retreat so that Bill and Karen can attend. I can never repay the debt I owe them for their kindness and support, but this is a start. I want it to be a surprise. I think that will add to the blessing."

As it turned out, Bill and Karen weren't the only ones to get a surprise blessing. One week later, on her birthday, Peggy got a call from her father, whom she hadn't seen in thirty years.

"When my dad left, I lost all contact with him. It took a while for me to find him, and since he lived so far away, we could only stay in touch by phone. My dad said that he and my stepmother wanted to give me $1,000 for my birthday. He's never done anything like that before. Linda, that's ten times more than I gave for my friends to attend the retreat. God is so awesome! I can't believe how he takes care of me," she beamed.

Polish Your Jewels:

- When your paycheck comes, write out a check to your church for ten percent of it, before you pay any other bill. Trust God to take care of the rest of your expenses (see Mal 3:10).

- Keep a journal of God's provision for you. Write down and date the stories of how God supplies your needs.

- Offer to share your testimony in your local congregation to inspire others to rely on God.

Day 15: Parenting

"Her children arise and call her blessed." (Prov 31:28)

Scripture Insight: There isn't a mother breathing who doesn't want her children to realize all she has sacrificed for them. And there isn't a mother of teenagers who thinks they ever will! Luckily, teenagers grow to adults and finally "get a clue." Sometimes, God grants them insightful moments along the way that make it all worthwhile.

The Mother Ship

The minute I found out I was pregnant with my first child, I headed to the nearest Christian bookstore and purchased several books on parenting. I didn't have a legacy of positive parenting, so I needed all the help I could find. Dr. James Dobson's *Dare to Discipline* and other books gave me tools to accomplish the daunting task of raising another human being. I studied how to deal with temper tantrums, bedtime drama, and homework hassles. But nothing could have prepared me for the turbulent teens.

I really thought that if I loved my children thoroughly, talked to them frequently, and encouraged them in the things they loved to do, we would avoid all the unpleasant door slamming and hair flipping that other parents experience. (You probably think I believe in the Tooth Fairy too, don't you?)

When my firstborn Sarah turned fourteen, a new era of parenting dawned. Suddenly, the parents she had once loved and respected became "so lame," by her definition. She decided that she could handle herself without our input and that all of our strict rules were patently unfair. Convinced that she was being held to a higher standard of behavior than her friends, she groaned, "It's just because I'm a pastor's kid." Then she would roll her eyes, flip her long blond hair behind her shoulder, and flounce to her room.

That's when I returned to Dr. Dobson's Web site, desperate for more instruction. Two illustrations in his book *Parenting Isn't for Cowards* captured my attention. The first showed a kid in a canoe, floating down a river. Along the bank were numbered signs corresponding to his age: 14, 15, 16…all the way to 19. But at the 17 marker, a torrential waterfall poured down and pounded the kid to death. That's what we parents think is going to happen, Dr. Dobson stated.

The second illustration showed what really happens. It portrayed the same kid in the canoe, floating peacefully through the teenage years. As he reached the year 17, there was indeed a hammering waterfall, but in this picture, the kid got soaked yet emerged to smooth sailing again. I tossed the book across the room. "Dr. Dobson doesn't know Sarah," I muttered. "She can be so stubborn!"

One afternoon shortly after her nineteenth birthday, as I was staining the trim on our new home, Sarah walked into the garage with a two-year-old in tow. "Well, who do we have here?" I asked, leaning down to make eye contact with a beautiful blue-eyed boy holding Sarah's hand.

"His name is Eric," Sarah said. "His mom is in my photography class at college. She likes my work and wants me to take his picture, so I brought him here to take advantage of our view. It's no use talking to him, Mom. Eric doesn't talk because his mother doesn't spend enough time with him. When I have kids, I'm going to quit my job and stay at home with them, like you. I'm going to talk with them about the flowers, trees, and God. I'm going to do it just like you did."

I couldn't believe my ears. My first thought was, *Where's the mother ship, and what have the aliens done with Sarah?*

My once-recalcitrant daughter continued to tout her plans to be a parent like me. I kept on staining the trim as I listened, afraid that if I stopped and looked her in the eye, she might realize what she was actually saying. Then she took little Eric by the hand and whisked him away to our deck so she could take his picture in front of the pine trees and star jasmine.

It turned out that Dr. Dobson was right. At nineteen, Sarah returned to the dimpled darling I once knew. Even though she had called me "lame," "unfair," and "old-fashioned," that day in the garage I finally heard her rise up and call me blessed. And you know, I believe I had earned it!

Polish Your Jewels:

- List what you are doing right as a parent. Save that list for the day your oldest child turns thirteen.

- As long as you have a teenager, read that list to yourself twice a day. Use it as positive self-talk when your teenager questions everything you do and say.

- Repeat what you said when you had one child on your hip and another one hanging onto your leg: "This too shall pass."

Day 16: Influence

"The tongue of the righteous is choice silver; the mind of the wicked is of little worth. The lips of the righteous feed many, but fools die for lack of sense." (Prov 10:20 NRSV)

....

Scripture Insight: Our words have great power to influence others. They can bring hurt or hope to those around us. If not for the kind words of the youth pastor who invited me to church when I was a teenager, I wouldn't be a Christian today. He brought light to my path, peace to my soul, and life eternally with Jesus.

Richard's Righteous Words

Being a fatherless family in the 1960s, we were considered very odd. Most people were leery of "those kids from that broken home." So you can imagine our surprise when Maude Gober (how's that for a good Southern name?), a neighbor across the street, came over and invited our family to church. She brought cupcakes. I thought, *Chocolate! I'm in!* Knowing my mother wasn't much for religion, I really didn't think she'd let us go. But she told Maude that she would have us ready and waiting the following Sunday. I suppose Mama thought she could bring retribution on those "holy-rollin' hypocrites," as she was fond of calling Christians, by sending her reprobate children to church. Curiously, that wasn't how those church people felt about us at all. They didn't treat us like brats. They treated us like blessings. It seemed surreal.

Mrs. Gray, my Sunday school teacher, took an interest in me the first day. She found out where I lived and made sure that I had a ride to church when Mrs. Gober couldn't bring me. Every week, she would teach a handful of us kids a Bible lesson that she had obviously spent a lot of time preparing. I couldn't quite figure out what was in it for her, but I told myself that I came for the cupcakes. Truth is, I showed up because this was the one place in the world where I felt someone cared about me.

The church sanctuary was quite an experience—so clean, peaceful, and reverent, completely unlike anything in my everyday world. I still remember sitting in that rock-hard maple pew in our little country church, hearing that deep-voiced, pulpit-pounding preacher talk about "getting saved." As a ten-year-old kid, I couldn't figure out who was drowning! But it only took a few Sundays for me to realize he was talking about me. I was drowning in a sea of emotional pain, loneliness, and separation from God.

Every Sunday, that preacher gave an altar call, and every Sunday I gripped the pew in front of me until my knuckles turned white, tears streaming down my face because I wanted to go forward. I wanted to give my life to Christ, but I just couldn't. Nothing would ignite my mother's wrath more than if I "got religion." And you know what they say: "If Mama ain't happy, ain't nobody happy." I wasn't sure what my brother would do if I became one of those "religious freaks." I didn't know how my twin sister would react. So, week after week, I came to church and felt God tugging on my heart. I wanted to ask Jesus to be my personal Savior. I wanted to have my sins forgiven. I wanted to be saved, but I wanted my family's approval more.

All through the week, I would think about the pastor's words. He said that Christ wanted me. *How can that be?* I thought. *Not even my mother wants me.* At least, it felt that way.

I prayed that nothing bad would happen to me until I could figure this out. I fantasized that if I was suddenly stalled on a railroad track, I would quickly pray, "God save me!" and he would. Or if I was falling off a tall building, I supposed I would blurt out, "Jesus save me!" and that would take care of things. (Remember, I was only ten years old.)

As time passed, I became too "cool" to attend school, much less church. I decided to be done with God, but he was not done with me.

In my eighth-grade year, that little church hired a youth pastor. Of all places in that little town where he could have lived, where do you think the Lord set him? Right down the street from our house.

Richard Smith was a thin man with kind eyes and a broad smile. He came by the house at least once a week to invite me back to church. When he didn't stop, he would honk his horn. To go anywhere in town, he had to pass our house, so every time he drove by, I would hear his shrill VW horn. I couldn't believe his persistence.

One Saturday afternoon, Richard showed up with a cute guy from the church youth group. This was better than Mrs. Gober's chocolate cupcakes! I figured I might as well go back to church. My life was already a mess, so what did I have to lose?

As I walked back into the church sanctuary that day, it felt like a safe place. I sat down in the freshly polished maple pew, rubbing my hand over the smooth wood as I slid across. I savored the slightly musty smell that I remembered from before. It gave me a sense of comfort. As the music began to envelop me, I became aware of what a sanctuary this place truly was for me. I realized I missed it.

It was the Sunday of the 1967 Arab-Israeli War and the same deep-voiced, pulpit-pounding preacher stood behind the podium. He gave an invitation so powerful that I think it would have made Billy Graham come to the altar. The only difference between this Sunday and all those when I had heard him before was that now I came to the altar, giving my life to Jesus Christ.

I often wonder where my life would have gone if it wasn't for Richard Smith's kind words and diligent invitations. Proverbs says that the lips of the righteous will feed many. Richard's words fed me then and will continue to feed me for eternity.

Polish Your Jewels:

- Think of those who influenced you to enter the kingdom of God. Thank God for bringing them into your life.

- Do your words "feed" those around you? If not, what could you do today to change that?

- To whom can you offer words of encouragement today? Whom can you invite to church this week?

Day 17: Trust

"Trust in the LORD with all your heart and lean not on your own understanding; in all your ways acknowledge him, and he will make your paths straight." (Prov 3:5–6)

....

Scripture Insight: Sometimes the Christian walk requires us to exercise our "trust muscle." Life can seem scary, even hopeless at times, but Proverbs tells us not to lean on our own understanding of the situation. We can look at our circumstances and feel intimidated, or we can look to Jesus and be empowered.

Harry Harlow's Monkeys

Our dad left our home when I was five, and my mother began waiting tables on the dinner shift at a nearby restaurant. When she wasn't working, she was either yelling at us or sleeping. Depressed people do that.

Mother's punishments never fit our crimes. It was crazy-making. I could hurl obscenities at the neighbors at the top of my lungs in the morning and go unpunished; but if I spilled milk at the dinner table that night, I might get beaten until my eyes swelled shut. Life in that broken-down monument to deferred maintenance that we called a home was miserable. It was easy to see why my father left. I wanted to leave too, but I was just a kid. So on those hot and sticky Southern nights, I would crawl up a mimosa tree in our front yard, wait for the lightning bugs to come out, and listen to the trains go by. I'd whisper to the whistling train to take me away, anywhere but here.

The Lord must have heard me. The day I gave my heart to Christ, my twin sister Bev was at the altar next to me saying yes to Jesus as well. We became more than sisters that day; we became fellow soldiers in a war, and we had no way of knowing then the battles we would face.

I would like to tell you that when we said yes to Christ, life became smooth sailing, but you would know that wasn't true. I feared my mother wouldn't be happy about our decision, and I was right. She did everything she could to discourage us from our faith, even forbidding us to go to church at times.

So Bev and I tried to be the perfect kids to avoid her anger. We cleaned the house, cooked the meals, and took care of our little brother. At school, we made straight As and excelled in band, winning accolades from everyone except Mama. No matter how hard we worked to excel, she could find something to complain about.

"Any idiot could remember to take wet clothes out of the washer. How stupid can you get?"

"What are you, blind? You can't see that cobweb? What's wrong with you?"

"You kids are just like your dad. You're not going to amount to anything."

"You're lucky you've got me, because nobody else would have you."

We did the best we could, but it was never good enough. Life at home felt hopeless. On those crazy days, Bev and I would talk late into the night just to stay sane. Many nights I cried myself to sleep and felt a hand patting me in the darkness and Bev's voice telling me it would be all right. A few nights later, I would hear Bev sobbing into her pillow, and it would be my turn to pat her and tell her things would be OK, although I didn't see how they ever could be.

Our little country church became our refuge. We were there every time the doors were open. One night, my youth pastor shared the scripture passage from Proverbs 3:5–6: "Trust in the Lord with all your heart; and lean not on your own understanding; in all your ways acknowledge him, and he will make your paths straight." I decided to commit this verse to memory and do my best to trust God, even though things did not seem to get any better.

School was a sanctuary too. Bev and I had a few classes together. One of them was sixth-period psychology class. One afternoon, the teacher gave us time to read the textbook section that described Harry Harlow's research on rhesus monkeys. Harlow placed baby monkeys in a cage with a choice of two fake monkey mothers. One was made of terrycloth; the other was made of wire with a milk bottle attached. His study revealed that the monkeys would cling to the terrycloth mother, foregoing food even to the point of starvation. When both fake monkeys were removed, the baby monkeys clung to each other for security.

This seemingly innocuous text moved me to tears and I couldn't help looking across the classroom at Bev. She was crying too. We didn't need to exchange words. We both realized that God had given us each other. We began to refer to ourselves as Harlow's "together together monkeys."

For the first time, I realized God had not left me alone. Despite our dismal circumstances, God had blessed Bev and me with each other, and he would prove trustworthy.

Today, Bev and her husband Tom run a successful Christian counseling practice and have written several books on relationships. I thank God every day for the privilege of serving him with my precious husband Bruce at our church near Yosemite National Park. The Lord graciously gave Bev and me beautiful children to love as we were never loved. God proved faithful. When we trusted him despite our circumstances, he did direct and straighten our paths.

Polish Your Jewels:

- Are you having difficulty trusting God for your future?

- Have you exercised your "trust muscle" lately? Every day, make a conscious decision to trust God in your circumstances.

- Memorize Proverbs 3:5–6, Psalm 37:4, and Jeremiah 29:11. Recite them to yourself when your faith seems weak.

Day 18: Guidance

"Commit to the LORD whatever you do, and your plans will succeed." (Prov 16:3)

....

Scripture Insight: After counseling others for sixteen years, I have noticed that most people either view God as a divine cop, ready to spoil their fun, or they see him as a cosmic genie, ready to grant their every request. Neither analogy is healthy or true.

We are blessed to be co-laborers in this world with our Creator. When we seek his will and follow his guidance, he brings joy, peace, and fulfillment to our lives. That's quite a plan for living!

Dare to Dream

Soon after I gave my life to the Lord in a little country church near Chattanooga, I started receiving a publication called *Student Tips* from Azusa Pacific College, a Christian school in California. It seemed too good to be true. I was sure that Azusa students must surf between classes (not realizing that the college was forty miles inland). Azusa seemed as far away as I could get from the craziness and dysfunction of my home life, so that's where I wanted to go!

Because I wanted to attend a Christian college, I applied myself to my studies and began to excel in my classes. My twin sister, Bev, shared this dream. We became serious high-school students and dared to dream of a life away from the constant abuse of our home.

One night when our mother wasn't in her usual irritable mood, we approached her about this idea. So much for her not being in an irritable mood! She told us that since our dad had left, she had to work—so we had to work. We had to take care of the cooking, dishwashing, laundering, house-cleaning, and babysitting our little brother.

"Mama's not about to give up her cheap labor," my sister said as we returned to our room. I knew Bev was right, so we quietly prayed about this. We asked our church youth group to pray with us too.

Not long afterward, both our youth pastor and senior pastor took new assignments. Church just didn't seem the same. Then one Sunday in my junior year of high school, a tall, slender man with the perfect timbre in his speaking voice stood up behind the pulpit and said, "My name is Everett Ashton. I'm your new pastor, and I am a graduate of Azusa Pacific College."

I know he must have said other things that morning, but that's all I heard. My sister and I tried to contain our excitement until the church service was over. Then we beelined to the pastor's office, flew through the door, and rattled off our story. After he calmed us down, he smiled kindly and said, "Don't worry, girls. Folks here at church have already told me all about your dedication to the Lord and your desire to go to a Christian college."

"They have?"

"I know the president of Azusa personally," the pastor continued. "I'll see that you get in."

A few short months later, Mama had a major meltdown and threw my sister and me out of the house. My sister called our dad and he came to get us. One minute I was living near Chattanooga, Tennessee, ready to graduate from high school with honors; the next minute I was in Charlotte, North Carolina, with a father I barely knew, a stepmother I had met only once, and a little sister I barely knew existed. *This can't be good,* I thought. *Charlotte is even farther away from California. I can kiss that dream good-bye.*

But my father was different from my mom. He wanted his girls to fulfill their dreams. "Y'all are smart," he commented at the dinner table one evening. "You need to do something with all those good grades you've earned. Where do you want to go to school? We have great schools around here like Duke and Vanderbilt."

This was our cue. Bev and I poured out our hearts about wanting to go to a Christian college. Azusa is a private college, more expensive than state schools; that made it an even harder sell. But our father loved us enough to support our dream. "I don't have any money to give you," he said, "but I'll help you fill out the paperwork to apply for a scholarship."

Six weeks after we sent off our applications, a letter arrived from Azusa Pacific College, addressed to Bev and me. I handed it to her because I was too nervous to be trusted with a letter opener!

Pastor Ashton had kept his word. The letter was from Dr. Cornelius Haggard, the president of Azusa. It read, "I talked recently with Everett Aston and he told me all about your desire to get a quality Christian education, and how hard you have worked toward your goal. I want you to know that you are just the kind of young people that we are looking for at Azusa Pacific. You are not only accepted but, with the work-study program, grants, and scholarships, your way is paid. The last $1,000 was supplied by a personal friend of mine from Hawaii—$500 for each of you. He too was moved by your story and determination. Welcome to California. We'll see you in the fall."

I spent four of the best years of my life at Azusa Pacific College (now University), graduating summa cum laude and meeting the love of my life there, my wonderful husband Bruce. I committed my way to the Lord, and he guided me to success.

Polish Your Jewels:

- Have you dared to dream large lately?

- What would you do for God if money was no object?

- Scripture says that God owns "the cattle on a thousand hills" (Ps 50:10). Ask him to butcher a few for your Kingdom endeavors.

Day 19: Priorities

"For wisdom is better than jewels; and all that you may desire cannot compare with her." (Prov 8:11 NRSV)

....

Scripture Insight: Max Lucado says that life is like climbing a ladder: You can get to the top, only to find out it's leaning against the wrong building. God had an unusual way of bringing that home to my son Jacob, causing him to reevaluate his priorities in life.

Hitting the Reset Button

Ever since my son Jacob picked up a guitar, he has seldom put it down. He had just started junior high school, so I'm sure the fact that "chicks dig musicians" has been one of the reasons. In addition, his dad was a master guitarist. Bruce has always astounded people with his ability to play, and Jake wanted to know everything his dad could teach him. If Bruce showed him a fancy guitar lick, Jake would sit in his room practicing it until he had it down cold. He got so good that when he was eighteen, he received a music scholarship to a leading university.

When Jake announced in his early twenties that he wanted to pursue a career in music, it came as no surprise to me. As my father used to say, "If you like what you do, you'll never work a day in your life!" I knew Jake had the talent to become a professional musician, but I also knew a lot of aspiring musicians starve before they become successful. Jake wanted to try to make it in Hollywood, where some musicians do succeed in their chosen profession but starve morally and emotionally. So I got on my knees to pray for my son's future.

Tinseltown turned out to be tougher than Jake expected. He played some lucrative gigs and some not so much, but he waited on tables, wrote music, and sang whenever he could. He found a great roommate, but when Jason moved out to get married, Jake wound up in a friend's garage. After a few months without air conditioning in that uninsulated garage, Jake called home.

"Dad, can I come home for a few months?" he asked. "I'll work a couple of jobs, save my money, and come back here with a cash reserve. I just need to press the reset button." His dad could hear the weariness in Jake's voice, and Bruce felt in his heart that God was in this decision.

The minute Jake got home, he was hired by a plumber in our church. He showed up on the job at five o'clock in the morning. He'd work all day, and many nights he'd wait tables at a four-star restaurant in our tourist town.

Jake saved his money and eagerly anticipated returning to Hollywood as soon as he could. While he was home, we got to enjoy our son. He got to write music inspired by the beauty of the mountains surrounding us.

With newfound inspiration, he decided to use some of his dad's recording equipment to create a music CD to sell online. He worked tirelessly on it. After a few months, his

CD was recorded and sent off for duplication, and he felt renewed. He was ready for the big city again.

During that time, Jake's faith got an overhaul as well, and his music reflected it. One day he asked what kind of Bible I would recommend. "I still have the student Bible you guys got me while I was in college," he said. "I'd like something different now."

"I like the *NIV Study Bible*, among others," I responded. "You've been such a help to me with getting my Web site up and running that I would love to buy one for you."

"Thanks, Mom, but I really believe I need to buy it for myself. That will make reading it more of a priority for me." After doing a good deal of research online, Jake placed his order.

Jake hadn't been in Los Angeles for long when the UPS driver walked up his driveway with a delivery. He had Jake's CDs, and on top of the box was his new Bible. "Mom, I ordered my Bible weeks after I sent my CDs for duplication," Jake told me on the phone, "but they both arrived the same day! I felt it was a reminder to put God first, before my career plans. Before I open this box of CDs and start selling my music, I need to open my Bible and see what God has to say about my life."

I couldn't have been more proud. My son could have climbed to the top of the *Billboard* chart with an empty soul and no amount of money would have satisfied him. But he chose to seek God instead, and that wisdom is better than jewels.

Polish Your Jewels:

- Take inventory of your priorities. Look at your checkbook and your daily planner to see what matters most to you.

- How do your life pursuits line up with what God says should be your top priorities?

- What choices do you need to make today to align with God's best for your life?

Day 20: Direction

"A man's steps are directed by the LORD. How then can anyone understand his own way?" (Prov 20:24)

....

Scripture Insight: I am so thankful that the Lord directs my steps. If I had been in charge of my life, who knows where I would have ended up? So many times, God has intervened to direct me where he wanted me to go, in spite of myself. Now when things are difficult to understand, I hang onto him in faith, because I know that clarity is just around the corner. When I trust the Lord, he always guides me.

"When Will You Get Serious?"

One of my all-time favorite jobs was working at the snack bar in college. I love people, and there were always a lot of them hanging around food on a college campus. I enjoyed meeting many of the off-campus students I normally wouldn't get to see as they grabbed breakfast each day. Bruce was one of them. He had a ready smile, gorgeous blue eyes, and a way of conveying that he really cared about anyone he was talking to. Somehow in the course of conversation, he often managed to say, "Linda, when are you going to get serious and go out with a theology student instead of those jocks you always date?" I thought Bruce might be expressing some real interest in me, but he never followed through, so I dismissed his question and talked about the weather.

One morning, the grill cook wasn't about to let that pass. "Yeah, Linda, when *are* you going to go out with Bruce?" he interrupted.

"Larry, he's never really asked me," I responded while looking at Bruce.

Undaunted, Larry the cook continued, "So, Bruce, are you asking her?"

By the look on Bruce's face, I could tell he hadn't expected anyone to call his bluff. "I guess so," came his stumbling response.

"When are you going out with him then, Linda?" Larry pressed.

"Tuesday night."

"What are you two going to do, Bruce?" Larry persisted.

"Dinner and a movie?" Bruce said it more as a question than an answer.

"Dinner and a movie OK with you, Linda?" Larry asked, still negotiating.

"Sure."

"What time are you picking her up, Bruce?"

"Six o'clock."

"He'll be there at six o'clock," Larry said, looking at me while handing Bruce his breakfast.

I had all but forgotten this humorous patter when I ran into Bruce at the library. "So do we have a date on Tuesday?" he asked, not sure whether we had really committed ourselves to Larry's arrangement.

"I guess so."

"See you at six o'clock then."

Bruce showed up at six o'clock on the dot. We looked through a newspaper for a movie but ended up talking so much that we didn't go. We covered everything from whether we thought God cried to the second coming of Christ.

Thirty-three years have passed and we still fill the hours with our conversations about faith, but also about kids and church growth. God knew we needed to be together, so he placed Larry the cook in exactly the right spot to make it a reality. If he hadn't been there with his amusing intervention that day, I might have missed one of my life's greatest blessings—a wonderful marriage to my best friend. God truly does direct our steps, even when we don't have a clue what's happening!

Polish Your Jewels:

- Think back on the landscape of your life. What were some times when you have seen God's hand directing you?

- Where might you be today if he had not presented those divine doorways?

- Has God ever placed you in circumstances that you didn't appreciate at the time but which turned out to be a blessing?

- Thank God for his provision and use the experiences of your past to bolster your faith in the future.

Day 21: Treasured Moments

"Direct your children onto the right path, and when they are older, they will not leave it." (Prov 22:6 NLT)

....

Scripture Insight: When my children were growing up, many things distracted me from parenting. I worried about whether other people would think my house was clean enough or suitably decorated. I fretted over whether I was wasting my college degree by not investing enough time in my career. I lay awake at night wondering why I couldn't be Superwoman like some of the other mothers I knew.

In retrospect, I wish I had worried less and enjoyed my children more. Yet God took care of them in spite of my distractions, and he even offered me an occasional "memorable mother moment" to confirm that.

Girls Gone Mild

I have two beautiful daughters. Their childhood was filled with fairy princesses, doll houses, and our personal favorite: tea parties. I bought my oldest daughter Sarah her first tea set on her third birthday. That same day, we filled the tiny plastic teapot with sweet tea, made bologna sandwiches with the crust cut off, and served banana chips with a dollop of peanut butter (Sarah's favorite). Then we sipped tea and chatted about the clouds, the flower garden, and our new puppy. Life couldn't get any better.

When Sarah was five, she was joined by her baby sister Ashley. We invited Ashley to join our tea parties when she was barely old enough to hold a cup. The three of us drank our tea with delight, even though Ashley's toddler table manners left much to be desired.

As the years progressed, so did the sophistication of our tea parties. About that time, a tea house opened in our little town, so there would be no more plastic dishes or paper plates for us. We had the real deal! At least once a month, I'd pick Ashley up after high school and we'd head over to the tea house for tea and scones in the early afternoon. Many times, we were the only customers in the place. Time stood still as Ashley and I talked about her future plans, classmates who were making disastrous choices, and whether Sarah's husband would be OK while he was stationed in Iraq. Those were deep and precious moments we treasured.

Ashley too grew up and headed off to college. During her spring break one year, I was blessed to have both girls home at the same time, Sarah from graduate school and Ashley from her second year at the university. This was a rare opportunity, so I headed to the grocery store to purchase food for a superb Easter feast.

When I returned, the girls asked me to follow them to the deck. There was the patio table set with my fine china, complete with linen tablecloth and napkins. The table was laden with cucumber-and-cream-cheese sandwiches, as well as banana chips frosted with peanut butter. The girls poured Blue Lady tea, and we laughed and talked until the sun set.

I felt so honored that, of all the places my girls could have gone during spring break, they chose to be with me. Apparently, I wasn't the only one who treasured those moments over tea.

Polish Your Jewels:

- Put down your book. Go sit on the floor and play with your children. No, I mean it. Put down the book.

- What, no children at home? Call one of your grandchildren and make a phone memory, or take a friend's child for an afternoon outing.

- Thank God for the relationships with children that he has given you.

Day 22: Foundation

"When the storm has swept by, the wicked are gone, but the righteous stand firm forever." (Prov 10:25)

....

Scripture Insight: The Lord provides a foundation of help through his Word. When disaster strikes us (and it will), he will use that foundation to show us that he's there and he cares.

Barb's Bible Verse

'll get it," I called over my shoulder as I lunged for the phone on a dreary December evening. It was the doctor from UCLA, calling with a date for our daughter's open-heart surgery. At five, Ashley had already survived two operations. The doctor closed the conversation by soberly stating, "Mrs. Newton, given the severity of her heart problems and with a surgery of this magnitude, I need you to prepare yourself *not* to take your daughter home." I felt my own heart skip a beat.

"Doctor, I help a lot of people deal with very stressful situations," I said. "But I have to tell you, I don't know how to do that myself." As I hung up the phone, fear crept over me like a dark cloud. I called my stepmother three thousand miles away and poured out my fears to her.

"Honey, I want to read you what the pastor shared last Sunday," Barb replied. As she left the phone to retrieve her Bible, I heard the Lord speak to my heart: *You prayed for your parents to accept me, didn't you? Now your stepmother is encouraging you with scripture. Did you ever know her to read the Bible before? You prayed for that too, didn't you? I heard your prayers then, and I will hear your prayers now.*

Barb returned to the line and read Isaiah 41:10 from *The Message*: "Don't panic. I'm with you. There's no need for fear for I am your God. I'll give you strength. I'll help you. I'll hold you steady, keep a firm grip on you." I felt the peace of the Lord saturate me as Barb read to me that night.

The next morning, as I entered a classroom full of fourth-graders, I noticed a card on my desk from one of my room mothers. "I don't know why, but the Lord laid you on my heart yesterday," she wrote. "I found this verse and I felt like it was for you." There in bold letters was Isaiah 41:10. The words spoke comfort to my soul again.

On my way home from school, I flipped on the car radio just in time to hear a Bible teacher say, "My text for this evening is Isaiah 41:10." Tears filled my eyes as I realized the Lord had gone to a lot of trouble to let me know he had prepared the way for my daughter and me. He had laid a foundation for our faith.

Polish Your Jewels:

- Write down a Bible verse that the Lord impressed upon you during a difficult time. What were you experiencing? How did this scripture help you?

- Find three other verses that provide this same kind of hope and commit them to memory.

- Send a card of encouragement to someone you know and include one of these verses.

Day 23: Wise Choices

"Wisdom is supreme; therefore get wisdom. Though it cost you all you have, get understanding. Esteem her and she will exalt you. Embrace her and she will honor you. She will set a garland of grace on your head and present you a crown of splendor." (Prov. 4:7–9)

Scripture Insight: When God offered King Solomon anything he wanted, he chose wisdom instead of wealth, power, or fame. Here Solomon encourages us to "esteem and embrace" wisdom. He says that we will wear the benefits of wisdom like a crown, a tiara for all to see. Now that's my kind of "bling from the King"!

Career Decision

Beverly Connor was a great doctor. Those of us privileged to have her as a pediatrician considered ourselves supremely blessed, especially when our children had special needs. Beverly had been recommended to us when our two-year-old daughter Ashley had her second heart surgery. Dr. Connor possessed the objectivity of a seasoned professional and the sensitivity of an experienced mother. More than once, she called me to say that her intuition told her to check on Ashley. Each time, we were about to call her because our child was manifesting odd symptoms. "Then bring her in. We'll take care of her," Dr. Connor would say.

One morning, as she was wrapping up Ashley's routine exam, she sank down onto a stool in the corner of the room. "Ashley checks out great, but I need to share something with you. I'm selling my practice," she said.

What will we do without Dr. Connor? I wondered. *She's in her prime. How can she give this up?* But all I could say was, "Why?"

"I'm going to stay at home with my children," came her firm reply.

"How old are they?"

"Six and twelve."

"Well, I guess kids at any age need their mom," I remarked.

"Oh, I'm not going home because my kids need me," she said. "I'm going home because I need them. My colleagues say I'm crazy. They say I'm giving up all I've worked to achieve in my field. But what is it worth if I miss enjoying my children? My practice probably will be here when I'm ready to return, and if it's not…well, that's a chance I'm willing to take."

It turned out the doctor was right. After nearly a decade of enjoying motherhood, she returned to medicine and within a few months she had more patients than she could handle. Dr. Connor made wisdom supreme in her life, though at the time it seemed to demand a high price. While others thought her foolish, she embraced wisdom and received a garland of grace. She enjoyed, with balance, all of the bounty that life had to offer her as a mother and a professional.

Polish Your Jewels:

- Have you ever done something you believed in although you received criticism and ridicule from others?

- Have you ever hesitated to make a decision you believed was right because you feared other people's criticism? What happened?

- Search the Scriptures for verses on courage and memorize them to empower you to make wise decisions.

- Ask God for the strength to make decisions based on your convictions, not the opinions of other people.

Day 24: Comfort

"A man finds joy in giving an apt reply and how good is a timely word!" (Prov 15:23)

....

Scripture Insight: My husband and I have often stood beside dear friends who are grieving. It's one of the most difficult times for me, yet I feel honored that people allow us to enter the sacred place of their pain. I have learned that most of the time words are inadequate because grieving people don't want platitudes. They just want the presence of someone who cares. The greatest comfort we can offer is just to hug them and stand beside them.

Quincey the Comforter

Growing up in a family that rescued many stray dogs, I had never experienced cat ownership. Then we moved our family to six acres in the California foothills. A friend from church warned that we were likely to encounter plenty of rattlesnakes there since we were the first people to build a home in that area.

"I think I can help you with that," Marlene volunteered. "I have two ten-week-old kittens that can help to patrol the place." Their half-wild mother had raised them outdoors, and when the kittens were barely able to walk, mama cat had taught them to hunt.

So Quincey and Nosey came to live with us in early fall, and soon they began to earn their keep. They hunted gophers, keeping my small lawn pristine. They discouraged any vermin that tried to take up residence in our outbuildings. One afternoon, I watched in awe through the bedroom window as they both danced around a rattlesnake, each step carefully orchestrated to avoid its deadly bite. The creature wore itself out striking at them, and within minutes was killed and eaten.

The cats wrestled for hours and slept together in what I called their "kitty-cat clot." The twin brothers would doze so intertwined that it was hard to tell where one left off and the other began. I would find them balled up together on the sunbathed patio chair, under the front porch, or in an abandoned box in the garage at night. The two were inseparable.

It was difficult to get close to them, but Nosey began to respond to us and eventually tolerated affection from the family members of his choice. Quincey remained wary of all humans and only conceded to being petted under duress, preferring the safety of his kitty-cat clot.

One night, Nosey didn't show up at bedtime. We'd had a heavy spring downpour, which made it difficult the search the area. Still, we combed the hillside, calling for Nosey until the wee hours of the morning. We hoped he had just gone on a long hunting expedition.

After two days with no Nosey, we had to conclude that the worst had happened. But Quincey confirmed it. On the third evening at bedtime, Quincey began crying inconsolably. He yowled and insisted on coming inside the house, a place he had detested before. We let him in and tried to comfort him, but he continued to cry. He finally jumped up on our bed, nestled between my husband Bruce and me, and howled himself to sleep. His actions were completely out of character for this wild cat.

"This is the last cat I would ever expect to want this much human attention," Bruce said. We wondered what we could do to ease the poor creature's pain, but we missed Nosey too, so we just grieved together.

This evening ritual continued for several weeks until Quincey's cries began to subside. After that, he darted in the back door every chance he got, but instead of diving into our bed each night, he would climb to the landing at the top of the stairs and watch us from that safe perch.

After a lengthy phone conversation with my twin sister one evening in which I learned that she had been diagnosed with cancer, I sat at the dining room table and began to sob. Immediately, Quincey made his way down the stairs toward me. I opened my eyes to see him gently pawing my legs. Without invitation, he hopped into my lap and began to purr. He curled up quietly in my arms until I had stopped crying. Then he jumped down and resumed his perch on the high landing. He had never done that before and has never done it since. It was as though Quincey knew the pain of being a twin and fretting over the condition of the one you've known since before birth, and he wanted to relieve my pain.

Quincey's attentive presence comforted me more than any words that could have been uttered. Now when I stand beside a grieving person, I remember Quincey's comfort. Better then words are actions that say, "I'm here for you and I care."

Polish Your Jewels:

- Have you ever felt helpless to comfort a friend or loved one? Don't feel that your words have to be perfect. Simply be attentive in the time of grief and realize that your presence is the best comfort you can offer.

- When you grieve for someone, don't you appreciate the presence of a caring friend?

Day 25: Radiance

"Joyful is the person who finds wisdom, the one who gains understanding. For wisdom is more profitable than silver, and her wages are better than gold. Wisdom is more precious than rubies; nothing you desire can compare with her." (Prov 3:13–15 NLT)

....

Scripture Insight: The writer of Proverbs urges us to seek God's wisdom above possessions, position, power, or prestige. By the world's standards, my father was successful, but something vital was missing until he gave his life to Christ. At the end of his life, the Lord made himself known with a light that brought comfort and peace, not just to Dad but to all of those around him.

Daddy's Light

My father had been battling cancer for five years when the doctors recommended hospice care. I knew I needed to pay him a visit while he was still aware that I cared enough to come.

When I arrived, it was obvious that my stepmother was exhausted from caring for him. So when my younger sister Renee came to town, we explained that we wanted her to take a day to rest. "The two of us can handle Daddy's care while you go home and sleep awhile. Otherwise, we'll be taking care of you!" Renee said. Barb agreed to take up our offer.

Daddy sat up for a while, but he was in a great deal of pain. Just before lunch, he wanted to lie down. Ren and I walked him across the room to his bed. After fluffing pillows and rearranging covers to make him as comfortable as possible, we moved to the couches at the far end of the hospice room to talk while Daddy slept.

Renee didn't hear him stir, but I did. Clutching his covers, he whispered, "I hate this!"

I walked back to my father's bedside. I took his hand and said, "Daddy, I'm so sorry that you hurt. I'm so sorry you are in this pain." Then I prayed out loud, "Lord, you know your son is hurting, and you promised that we could come to you and you would give us rest. Let him rest in your arms of peace right now."

I felt a permeating sense of peace. Then I heard Renee speak. "Lin, look," she said. She was standing on the other side of Daddy's bed, holding his other hand. As I opened my eyes, I saw a brilliant ray of light radiating between us and resting gently upon my father. His brow that had been furrowed by pain was now relaxed. He slept serenely, enveloped in the glow. Ren began to pray out loud for Dad. When she finished, I started again. I don't know how long we remained in that sacred moment.

We were interrupted by a knock at the door. It was a longtime family friend who had come to visit. We ushered him to the sitting area of the hospice room so that Daddy could sleep while we talked. Our visitor didn't stay long, and the minute he walked out the door, Ren jumped up and said, "Could you believe that light? I'm so glad you were here, Lin, because no one would believe me if I told them. I'm not sure I would believe myself!"

"I'm glad I was here too," I agreed.

Just then Renee's husband Bill joined us. She quickly told him what had happened. From the way Bill rolled his eyes, I could tell he didn't believe her. Bill is a wonderful Christian man who is an airline pilot, and he is skeptical about emotionalism. Turning on his heel, he walked over to the window next to Dad's bed. Then he returned to the sitting area, wide-eyed with amazement.

"You know something? There's a building in front of that window," Bill reported, shaking his head.

"I know," I replied. "You can't say it was just the sun shining through the window and explain it away as some natural occurrence."

Bill was silent as he let this soak in.

My stepmother returned from her day of much-needed rest, accompanied by my twin sister. We left Bill to watch Dad while we crossed the hall to a kitchen where some Christian volunteers brought in meals for the hospice families each week. As we ate, Ren recounted our experience of praying for Dad and seeing him enveloped in light. "This radiance was bright yellow and glowing," she said. We both struggled for an adequate description of what we had seen.

Though my father had not become a Christian until late in life, I believe that Christ came to him in that hospice room as a radiant light to bring him rest and comfort. He brought all of us peace.

Polish Your Jewels:

- Have you ever experienced God's presence in a palpable way? What was happening in your life at the time?

- What did your experience teach you about the nature of God?

- Write down your own account of what you experienced so you don't forget how God revealed himself to you.

Day 26: Stillness

"Better a dry crust with peace and quiet than a house full of feasting, with strife." (Prov 17:1)

....

Scripture Insight: Despite the fact that our culture urges us to acquire all of the "toys" we can get, many discover too late that possessions aren't enough. I constantly see people in my counseling office who have worked themselves into a materialistic obsession that has left their souls bereft of peace. We could do with fewer things and more serenity.

Psalm 46:10 explains the significance of slowing down: "Be still and know that I am God." The Hebrew word for "still" in Psalm 46 is *raphah*. It means to slacken or cease; to be faint, feeble, or idle; to leave alone or let go; to draw toward evening. The root word for *raphah* is the Hebrew word *rapha*, which means to mend by stitching, to make or cause to heal or repair, to be made thoroughly whole. So here God is saying, "Sit down. Be quiet. Be at peace so I can make you thoroughly whole."

Twilight Reflection

On those hot, sticky summer nights of my childhood, after my mother had gone to her waitress job, I would climb into the mimosa tree in our yard to wait for the sun to go down. That's when the lightning bugs came out, and it was the most peaceful time of the day. Time seemed to stand still. Nothing in the world mattered except how many fireflies had yellow lights and how many had brilliant green ones. Even the bugs moved slowly, as if they understood the reverence of the moment.

In the original Hebrew for Psalm 46:10, the word for "still" can be translated "wait for evening." It suggests the image of sitting on your front porch with no agenda but to sip your sweet tea and watch the lightning bugs.

If I had a mimosa tree in my California yard, I'd still try to climb it. However, I do have a front-porch swing, and when I take the time, God meets me there. I find it difficult to slow down. However, since my soul starves for peace, I've learned some methods that help me to be still. They work for me, so perhaps they will help you too.

First, I take a deep breath and mentally evaluate all the mental clutter that keeps me from connecting with Christ. I see my right hand raking away all the things still undone for my family: the bills that need to be paid, the items I forgot to get at the grocery store, and the ever-growing nest of dust bunnies under every piece of my furniture. In my mind's eye, my left hand rakes away all the things left to accomplish at work: phone calls that need to be returned, reports to be completed, and deadlines looming over my head. I let God have all of the things that create noise in my mind so I can settle down and hear from him. Then I'm free to turn my attention to the "still, small voice" of God.

Next, I spend a few minutes praising God for his goodness. This swings open the door to his throne room, where I have the privilege of sitting at his feet. There I hear him say, *Hush, child. Hush now while I heal you.*

There are no lightning bugs in California, but that doesn't keep me from the white rocker on my front porch. If you'll excuse me, I believe I have an appointment there.

Polish Your Jewels:

- What keeps you from spending quiet time in the Lord's presence? Take an inventory of the barriers that keep you from intimacy with God. Ask him to remove them.

- Plan regular times to sit quietly in God's presence. Try the method mentioned above to still your mind. Spend as much time listening to the Lord as you do talking to him.

Day 27: Envy

"My fruit is better than fine gold; what I yield surpasses choice silver." (Prov 8:19)

....

Scripture Insight: Sometimes what we get from the Lord is not at all what we expect. However, he knows what's best for us, and his gifts (his "fruit") will always satisfy.

As the Deer…

My sister and her family were coming for a visit, and we were looking forward to a much-needed time of relaxation. They arrived with good news: Their offer to purchase a brand-new four-thousand-square-foot home had been accepted. Suddenly, the weekend wasn't quite so relaxing.

As we sat by the pond in front of our rental house, watching the kids swim, my sister told me about her plans to decorate their new place. I was genuinely happy for her, but inside I heard another line of reasoning: *Your sister gets her dream home and you get to go through another gut-wrenching surgery with your daughter. How fair is that? After all that you do for God in the ministry, can't he answer that simple prayer?*

I felt guilty about having such thoughts. At the same time, I dreaded what was around the corner for Ashley and me. As evening fell, the kids got tired and came inside. I told my sister that she could have the shower first. I was going to sit by the pond and enjoy the quiet for a few minutes before I had to pick up the house after five energetic kids. As the sun slipped from view behind an evening cloud, I tearfully poured out my frustration to the Lord. As I lifted my head to wipe my eyes, I saw him.

Standing less than twenty feet from me on the opposite side of the pond was the most magnificent buck I had ever seen. He had a huge rack of antlers and big brown eyes. Here I sat on a bright floral lounge wearing a florescent-colored bathing suit—all of which should have frightened him—but he just stood there, looking at me. I immediately thought of the words of the worship song "As the Deer," which says:

I want You more than gold and silver,
> only You can satisfy.[1]

The song is based on Psalm 42, which says, "As the deer pants for streams of water, so my soul pants for you, O God." In a moment, I knew the Lord heard my cry. A palpable sense of the Lord gave me peace. My daughter was facing a risky surgery, but I had the assurance that God would be with both of us.

---

1. "As the Deer," music and lyrics by Martin J. Nystrom, ©1984 by Maranatha Praise, Inc.

Polish Your Jewels:

- Make some time to sit alone in God's presence and wait quietly for him. How is he showing you that he cares, regardless of your circumstances?

- Write a list of all that God is doing for you today. Focus on this divine fruit, not on your problems.

Day 28: Surprise

"The hope of the righteous ends in gladness, but the expectation of the wicked comes to nothing." (Prov 10:28 NRSV)

....

Scripture Insight: Often when I'm discouraged, God provides a little gift in the midst of my discouragement—an inspiring word, a phone call from a friend, or an uplifting e-mail. In my daughter's case, he gave an unexpected gift to inspire her hope.

Grandma's Ring

At age fourteen, Ashley began to feel she was an unlucky girl. Young teen girls often do, but Ashley had more than her share of reasons to think it. Having just completed her fourth heart surgery, she had a bright red scar running from just under her neck to her navel. There were scars all over her body from drainage tubes and cut-down IVs, creating unevenness in places that needed symmetry. Shopping for a swimsuit was "the single worst experience of my life," she said. "They knocked me out during surgery, but I'm fully awake for this nightmare."

Ashley felt overwhelmed by the hand life had dealt her. Then came the day our family gathered to sort through some of Grandma's things.

After four years of suffering from dementia, my husband's mother had died and we had the daunting task of cleaning out her home. Mom was an avid yard-sale shopper, and she had accumulated rooms full of stuff to prove it. One thing she especially loved to collect was jewelry, and she left several cartons of it to sort.

My brother-in-law Clark suggested we gather all the family members and have each one take a turn choosing a favorite item. We would start with the youngest and work our way to the oldest person in the room, repeatedly choosing items until all of Grandma's bling had a home.

As the youngest grandchild, Ashley got first choice. She selected an owl necklace, one of Grandma's favorites, to remind her of her grandmother. Then the next cousin chose, and so on. After about the sixth round, we realized we had made scarcely a dent in the collection, so we decided that each person had to pick three things at a time. By now, everyone was choosing for everyone else in an effort to expedite the process.

On Ashley's turn, her twenty-eight-year-old cousin Jessica pointed to a small silver pinkie ring. "Look at this, Ash. Silver is in style these days, and I think you are about the only one of us with fingers small enough to wear this." She handed Ashley a ring that was caked in dust and talcum powder. "We found this in the bottom of one of Grandma's toiletry bags," she added. Ashley slipped the ring on her finger and it fit perfectly.

That evening, we soaked the ring in jewelry cleaner and Ashley put it on before dinner. As I sat across the table from my daughters, I noticed they both had their chins resting on their hands, with Sarah's diamond wedding ring next to Ashley's new find. "Girls, your rings have the same sparkle," I commented. They pulled off their rings and began to compare them. It was clear their stones had far more luster than my cubic zircon.

"Ashley should have this ring appraised," Sarah informed us. "She really doesn't know what she has here."

The next day was busy at the mall, but an elegant lady at Rogers Jewelry agreed to look at the ring. "I'm not an appraiser, but I can tell you what this is."

"Awesome. That would be a big help," Ashley said.

She took the ring from my daughter. After a few minutes, she returned with the ring and a jeweler's loupe. "Where did you get this ring?" she asked. Ashley told her the story of sorting through Grandma's bling.

"Well, you're one lucky lady," she informed Ashley. "This ring is not made of silver; it's white gold, and the diamonds are *real*! Both stones are of high quality and a rare cut that jewelers did around the 1920s. The small stones around them are quality diamond chips. Where did your grandmother get it?"

"We don't know," Ashley reported. "None of us ever saw her wear it. My cousin found it in the bottom of a cosmetic bag, covered in powder and goo. We think Grandma probably bought it at a yard sale."

"That's amazing!" the woman exclaimed. "We don't see many stones like this anymore. The rarity of the cut and the clarity of the diamond will increase the ring's value. Here's the name of an appraiser. I suggest you take it to him right away."

After hearing the story of the ring's origin, the appraiser informed my daughter that it was worth $3,500. "These diamonds are rare and valuable," he said. "You're one lucky girl!"

Out of three big boxes of costume jewelry, Ashley received the only thing of any real monetary value. The sparkle of her ring was nothing compared to the sparkle that returned to her big blue eyes!

Polish Your Jewels:

- Has some disappointment caused you to give up on God?

- Trust God and watch how he shows up to bless you in unexpected ways.

Day 29: Legacy

"A good name is more desirable than riches; to be esteemed is better than silver and gold." (Prov 22:1)

....

Scripture Insight: At funerals I have attended, I have never heard anyone discuss how much money the deceased made, what kind of expensive foreign car he drove, or where she bought her fine clothes. Family members and friends talk about how much that person made them feel loved and valued. So why do we work so hard to accumulate possessions rather than learning to appreciate people?

Our Own Santa Claus

The name Santa Claus brings a smile even to the most scowling Scrooge. I had the privilege of knowing Santa personally. It's true!

A couple of months after my husband and I came to this pastorate in the California mountains, God sent Dean and Irena Baker to our church. With a long silver beard, twinkling eyes, and cherry-red cheeks, Dean would don a red suit each Christmas and look like he had just stepped out of *The Miracle on 34th Street.* A woman spotted him while she was on vacation and was so impressed that she hired him to be Santa for three years in a row at an upscale mall in New Jersey.

My kids fell in love with the Bakers and quickly adopted them as surrogate grandparents. Our church initially met on a campground, and nearly every Sunday after the worship service, Dean would lead my kids over the campus on nature walks. With his red-and-green suspenders and Bermuda shorts ("Santa's off-season attire," he told them.), Dean would wander the landscape with three children in tow, explaining which trees would lose their leaves, where squirrels hid their nuts, and what kind of bird lost a certain feather they found along the way.

My younger daughter, Ashley, was particularly impressed with Dean. As we were ready to leave church, she would come running with a fistful of feathers and tell us what Dean had taught that afternoon. (She nearly came to blows with a boy in her third-grade class who insisted there was no Santa Claus. "Yes, there is!" she stamped her foot. "He goes to my church!")

Every year, clad in his custom-made Kris Kringle suit, Dean delighted kids at our church parties and programs. He also visited dozens of hospitals, retirement homes, long-term care facilities, and the homes of shut-ins, embodying the love of Christ as he spread Christmas cheer. Everywhere he went, folks fell in love with him.

When Ashley had major surgery, Dean and Irena drove five hours to visit her at the medical center. When she spotted her own personal Santa walking into the room, I saw the only smile that crossed her lips during her ten-day hospital stay.

Even after Dean was diagnosed with a rare blood cancer, he continued to bless people. He spent one more Christmas at the mall in New Jersey. Among all the kids who came to see him there, an elderly woman with a walker made her way through the line. She explained to Dean that her husband was in a local hospital's intensive-care unit. He always loved Santa, so she thought seeing a picture of her with jolly old St. Nick might cheer him up. Dean asked his store elves to stop the line while he prayed with the woman about her husband. He might have gotten fired for this, but he knew the woman needed compassion and prayer more than anything else. Instead of being scolded, Dean was commended by the management after they received so many letters thanking them for what he'd done.

Whether helping a friend build a garage with his carpentry skills, calling to encourage an ailing neighbor, or asking yet another child what he wanted for Christmas, Dean Baker loved the people around him. At his funeral, people from all walks of life came to the microphone to share how Dean had blessed them with his positive attitude and love. I've seldom witnessed a memorial service that was such a celebration. Dean left a legacy of love to everyone who crossed his path.

Polish Your Jewels:

- Have you known anyone whose life you wanted to emulate? Describe the person's attributes that you admire.

- How many of these traits are listed among the fruit of the Spirit? For example, Galatians 5:22–23 says, "The fruit of the Spirit is love, joy, peace, patience, kindness, goodness, faithfulness, gentleness and self-control. Against such things there is no law."

- Make a list of the spiritual fruit that you would like to see more evident in your own life.

- Pray for the life traits you desire. Surrender yourself daily to the Holy Spirit, allowing him to bear this fruit in you.

Day 30: Values

"My child, keep your father's commandment, and do not forsake your mother's teaching. Bind them upon your heart always; tie them around your neck." (Prov 6:20–21 NRSV)

....

Scripture Insight: As parents, we do our best and leave the rest to the Lord. But despite our best efforts, our children may not appear to embrace the values we've worked so hard to teach them. We need to remain diligent, because most values are caught, not taught, and our children may be "catching" more than we realize.

Janine's Inheritance

"You go to Sierra Pines Church, too," Janine commented as I sat in her chair, getting my hair trimmed. "So many people have invited me to that church."

"Well, add my name to that list," I replied.

As the stylist cut my hair, she told me about a retreat she was planning for her recovery group. *What a tireless volunteer!* I thought. During our conversation, I learned that Janine had been raised by devoted Christian parents. Her father John was a Christian school principal and her mother Pat was a faithful volunteer in their local church, working with everything from kids to craft classes.

That's where Janine learned her commitment to service, I concluded.

I was partly right.

"I've been clean and sober for four years now," she volunteered. "In order to keep what I've got, I have to give it away."

"I would love for our ladies' group to hear you," I said. "Would you come to my house for our next meeting to share your story with our group?" I almost felt presumptuous asking her so soon after we had met, but Janine had a delightful way of making me feel as if I had known her for years.

The ladies at the meeting enjoyed Janine's keen mind and quick wit, just as I had. She became part of our planning team. As we spent more time together, more of her story unfolded.

"I knew my parents loved me, but in my teenage years I grew to hate my mother," she said. "She knew I was messing up, and she did her best to call me on it. I wanted to do my own thing. I didn't want her cramping my style. So I grew more clever at finding ways to get away with my crazy behavior.

"I started drinking to look cool for my friends in high school," she continued. "It wasn't long before I realized that I was one of those people who *really* liked drinking. I liked the buzz. I felt it gave me courage. I even liked being drunk because I could medicate the pain of not being thin, smart, pretty, or popular."

Janine explained that "at first you have alcohol; then alcohol has you. I was out there for thirty years before I hit my bottom, and the entire time my parents continued to love me, despite my insane behavior. My dad never turned his back on me even though I know I broke his heart. My mom kept praying for me even though I continued to make poor choices.

"The day I found myself in a heap realizing I couldn't go on, they were the first people I called. There was no 'I told you so' or 'It's about time,' just genuine love that I was done with the insanity.

"A friend had been inviting me to a recovery meeting for months. Now I knew I had to go. I realized through the program that I never really lost faith in God. In fact, my recovery group helped me to reconnect with him. He is the higher power who keeps me sober from day to day. Now I want to give back to him for all he has given to me."

One day, I said, "Janine, you've only been back in church a short while, but you have the commitment of someone who has known the Lord for decades. Your parents raised you right!"

"They did, didn't they?" she replied.

Several weeks later, she told me of a conversation she had with her parents. "Linda commented about my Christian commitment," she told them, "and we both realized that you guys get a lot of credit for that. The faith you layered on me years ago kept me alive when I was drinking. It keeps me focused now. Thanks, Mom and Dad, for not giving up on me and for loving me back to Jesus."

King Solomon instructs us to bind our parents' wisdom around our necks. Janine did, and it's a necklace that will sparkle for eternity.

Polish Your Jewels:

- Do you have children or grandchildren for whom you are praying? Don't give up on them, no matter what they are doing.

- Find a friend who has a burden like yours and agree to pray together for your children.

- Pray for someone to come into your children's lives to show them Jesus Christ.

Day 31: Character

"A wife of noble character who can find? She is worth far more than rubies. Her husband has full confidence in her and lacks nothing of value. She brings him good, not harm, all the days of her life…She makes coverings for her bed; she is clothed in fine linen and purple. Her husband is respected at the city gate, where he takes his seat among the elders of the land. She makes linen garments and sells them, and supplies the merchants with sashes. She is clothed with strength and dignity; she can laugh at the days to come."
(Prov 31:10–12, 22–25)

....

Scripture Insight: Attending a Christian college in the seventies, my girlfriends and I had the words of Proverbs 31 decoupaged and hanging on our walls. This was the standard to which we all aspired. But truth be told, the lady of Proverbs 31 really intimidated me. She was far too industrious, capable, and "together." In no way could I ever measure up to her. Finally, I realized that the only way I could come close to her level of excellence was to allow the Holy Spirit to change me.

A Woman of Character

Linda, our church is hosting a luncheon and we'd like you to be our speaker. I've invited six other churches in town, so we're expecting about two hundred women. Can you make it?" Darlene, an energetic pastor's wife, suggested a date.

"I'm available that day and I wouldn't miss it!" I responded. "I think it's great that you are including several congregations. I'll mark my calendar."

"We'll see you in a couple of months."

I love speaking before women's groups, but I was especially delighted with Darlene's idea to build unity in her community. I looked forward to the event, praying, planning, and preparing.

The evening before the luncheon, I gassed up my car. I placed my notes and my Bible on a table next to the front door so I would be ready to head out and get to the church in plenty of time. Since I was traveling through Fresno, I decided to take a catalog order back to a department store there and save a trip later. I patted myself on the back for thinking ahead and making good use of my time.

In the closet, I found the heels I was planning to wear with my springtime ensemble. *Since I have to drive for nearly two hours, I'll just wear my Birkenstocks in the car and slip my dress shoes on later*, I thought. I felt so organized and put together as I placed my shoes next to the rest of the stuff I was taking.

The next day, bright and early, I got dressed in my best spring outfit, piled my things in the passenger seat, and headed down the road feeling like a perfectly prepared Proverbs 31 woman. While cruising down the road toward my destination, I glanced at the shoebox sitting neatly beside me and a sinking feeling came over me. I knew how distracted I can be when I get home from church. I often throw my clothes into the closet and pitch my shoes into any box available. I hadn't checked this box before I grabbed it the previous night. So I opened the box and, sure enough, it held blazing purple pumps. There I sat in my pale pink dress with a pale pink linen jacket and white nylons. Those were the wrong shoes!

Be resourceful, I thought. *There's a K-Mart just down the street from the church. I'll just pull in, lay down my credit card, and grab any pair of shoes that will work. Fashion before function. This should work.*

I turned off the freeway and pulled into the K-Mart parking lot. The store was empty! A faded imprint of the name still showed on the vacant building. So I slipped on my purple shoes and drove to the church.

I had to share with my audience what had happened. We all got a good laugh out of it. A precious little blue-haired granny hobbled up to me after the luncheon and said, "Honey, I *like* your purple shoes!"

The amazing Proverbs 31 woman is still my inspiration, but as you can see, when I'm "clothed in purple" (v 22), it's probably by mistake. And while I "laugh at the days to come" (v 25), I'm usually laughing at my mistakes. I haven't stopped holding her up as my example, but I have stopped beating myself up emotionally when I fall short. I've learned that God loves me, purple shoes and all.

Polish Your Jewels:

- Have you ever felt discouraged by some of the standards presented by the people of the Bible?

- List some of the character qualities of the Proverbs 31 woman that you desire. Keep them in your prayers and seek the Holy Spirit's power to gain them.

- Be patient with yourself.